HOW TO GET A DIVORCE WITH OR WITHOUT A LAWYER

David I. Levine

HOW TO GET A DIVORCE WITH OR WITHOUT A LAWYER
A Bantam Book / May 1979

ISBN 0-553-12407-2

Published simultaneously in the United States and Canada

Bantam Books are published by Bantam Books, Inc. Its trade-
mark, consisting of the words "Bantam Books" and the por-
trayal of a bantam, is Registered in U.S. Patent and Trademark
Office and in other countries. Marca Registrada. Bantam
Books, Inc., 666 Fifth Avenue, New York, New York 10019.

PRINTED IN THE UNITED STATES OF AMERICA

A NOTE FROM THE AUTHOR

The purpose of my book is to give you all the most practical and useful information available on divorce—what the law is, what the tax rulings are, and what emotional problems you may have to face.

I do not advocate divorce. But I do strongly advocate that you learn as much as you can about its legal, tax, and emotional ramifications. You will not only be better equipped to deal with any legal problems that might arise, but, more importantly, you will have a better chance of avoiding the helplessness, frustration, and anger that usually accompany the trauma of divorce.

—David I. Levine

This book is dedicated to Barbara and Dodi, my first and second wives, the two most talented women I have known. Barbara was a talented wife, a talented mother, and a talented artist. Dodi's one talent was that she got me for more money in less time than I have ever known any woman to get out of any man.

Publishers' Note

The reader should note that this book mainly offers general information on common problems relating to the matrimonial field, and does not purport to give personal, legal, or any other form of professional advice on any *specific* problem. The reader, therefore, should not assume that the information provided in this book is applicable or suited to his or her problem or circumstances in particular. Many factors need to be considered before a final course of action can be recommended to an individual. Accordingly, the reader should consult with his or her own professional attorney and accountant concerning particular circumstances before embarking upon any course of action in this area. Note, especially, that general statements on legal situations may not be applicable in every state, and the reader is advised to see his or her attorney for individual consultation concerning the nature of the law in the reader's state.

The state-by-state data of chapter 29 have been confirmed through correspondence with the respective state attorneys general's offices. But it should be noted that state laws frequently change and that, in this respect too, legal advice on current legislation should be sought.

Contents

Introduction

There is nothing more wonderful in this world than marriage—if it works. Raising a family is the nearest thing to godliness. Creating children, enjoying them and suffering along with them, watching them grow and develop, is the most beautiful experience two people can share, and anyone who misses it has missed an important part of life.

On the other hand, there is hardly anything more traumatic, bitter, and terrible than divorce. Recent statistics predict that one out of two persons who get married are going to be divorced. At the rate divorces are increasing, it could rise to 90 out of 100.

The only thing that qualifies me to write this book is that I have made more mistakes in dating, marriage, and divorce than most, and yet I have managed to survive financially, physically, and emotionally.

I do not advocate divorce; I do not advocate marriage; I do not advocate alternatives to marriage. But I do strongly advocate that you learn as much as you can about the legal, tax, and emotional aspects of these options so that you will be better equipped to cope with the problems that accompany them.

There is more interest in the subject of marriage and divorce than any other. And yet there is so little knowledge about it.

This book intends to fill that void.

It makes no difference whether we are wealthy or poor, old or young, male or female, educated or illiterate; it makes no difference what type of work we do. Once we become involved in a divorce action, we are all equals: helpless, unknowing, unhappy, and frustrated.

CASE IN POINT: In the past few months I have met several women whose husbands have sued for divorce. These women were not aware that, in their states, they could petition the court for separate maintenance (money with which to substain themselves) until final determination of their divorce actions. The appalling fact is that every one of these women had attorneys who presumably represented them, but who failed to inform them of a basic right and necessity. To me this inattention constitutes negligence and justifies the increasing number of suits for damages that are being instituted against lawyers.

CASE IN POINT: Recently the wealthy president of a well-known national corporation called me to discuss his divorce. He and his wife had separated longer than the two years required by his state for a no-fault divorce, but no progress had been made toward the property settlement, which involved millions of dollars. I asked him if he lived in a community property state. *He did not know.* I advised him to dismiss his corporate lawyer, who was also handling his divorce, and to employ the best divorce attorney available.

CASE IN POINT: A national magazine for single parents recently published an article by a divorced attorney whose own practice includes divorce litigation. He admitted that in spite of his experience as a lawyer, his knowledge of court procedures and local practices, his familiarity with lawyers in his area, his knowledge of the law, and his respect for the judge who heard his contested action, when he got a divorce he at times (1) felt that he had chosen the wrong attorney to represent him, (2) questioned his attorney's conduct of the divorce action, (3) felt the same tension induced by the pretrial hearing on support that he had observed in his clients, (4) dreaded the eventual outcome of sharp disputes, and (5) severely criticized the judge's decisions.

Which proves that even a lawyer is human when he becomes a client.

One peculiar phenomenon of divorce is that almost always, neither the husband nor the wife is satisfied with the results of the divorce proceedings. Over and over you hear "That's a shame . . . the law is unfair . . . the tax rulings are unfair . . . the judge is prejudiced . . . husband was wrong . . . lover was wrong . . . I shouldn't have trusted my lawyer," and the like. Even if the wife is given a generous award, she may feel cheated because she cannot have the husband she still loves. So she turns on her lawyer, his lawyer, and the judge. Or if the husband's alimony and child-support payments are high and he no longer loves his ex-wife, he often feels that he has been used by her, by both his lawyer *and* hers, *and* by the courts.

A major cause of this antagonism toward the legal establishment is the use of the adversary system in marital actions, which encourages lawyers to make every proceeding a battle. (The resentment widely felt against lawyers and judges has led to movements to eliminate them entirely from marital actions, and particularly from matters concerning children. While such a change might be helpful in the future, it will not help you today.)

The purpose of this book is to tell you *what* the law is, *what* the tax rulings are, and *what* emotional problems you may be facing. I cannot tell you what to do. But once you realize that many others have experienced similar problems and that you can learn how they have successfully coped with these problems, you can decide what *you* want. This book, I hope, will help you attain your goals with the least possible financial and emotional strain.

It was out of this concern that I spent over $100,000 of my own money to rent Madison Square Garden in New York City for an eight-hour-long free lecture on marriage and divorce (October 23, 1976). The questions treated in this book—in particular those in the Q-and-A passages—are the questions I was asked most often during that lecture and later on television and radio talk shows and in my extensive correspondence.

My editor at Bantam Books, Walter Glanze, has dubbed me "the Dr. Spock of marriage and divorce." I would be very proud if I filled the bill.

My first wife and I had two children who were raised on Dr. Spock. Every time she was puzzled by a physical condition of either child, she would go to the index to identify the symptom. If she learned it was typical of what happened to children of that age, she was immediately relieved because she realized that our problems were not unique.

Along with a diagnosis, Dr. Spock sometimes suggested a remedy used by thousands of others to treat a particular ailment. This is the same type of help I hope to give people with their legal, tax, and emotional problems in marriage and divorce.

From my experiences and observations, I'd like to give you first this general advice:

Try to forget the past. Do not dwell on it. It is not going to do you any good to concentrate your thoughts on how badly your former lover, husband, wife, or lawyer treated you. Don't build up that wall that so many millions of unhappy people have built. Condition yourself to be able to state with confidence that you have survived and overcome your past experiences, both good and bad.

Enter each new relationship with enthusiasm.

For the sake of brevity, when the term "man," "male," "husband," "he," and "him" are used, they refer usually to the spouse who will be paying money to the other party as alimony, child support, and so on. Likewise, when the terms "woman," "female," "wife," "she," and "her" are used, they refer usually to the spouse who is receiving such payments. If, in your case, the circumstances are reversed, simply reverse the terms.

PART ONE

The Divorce Action

1

How to Deal with Lawyers

Do I need a lawyer?

Professor Irwin Corey once said: "Roosevelt proved that you can be President forever; Truman proved that anybody can be President; Eisenhower proved that we don't need a President in the first place."

Do you need a lawyer in the first place? If you don't need a lawyer in order to marry, why do you have to have a lawyer for a divorce?

I mailed a questionnaire to the Attorney General of every state. One of the questions I asked was: "Can a couple in a no-fault situation visit the local Clerk of the Court and, with his help, fill out the necessary papers for divorce without using an attorney?

Answers I received ranged from a flat no to a definite yes. Examples:

1. "In Alabama there is a constitutional right to represent oneself in court. Therefore, a couple could handle its own divorce. But how many people are able to do this? Obviously, everything depends on the individuals involved. Can they get help from the clerk? Again, this depends on the willingness and the ability of the clerk. So the answer to your question is neither yes nor no, but maybe."

2. "In this state [Washington] the ability of a couple in a no-fault divorce situation to obtain assistance from the Clerk of the Court in filling out necessary papers varied from county to county. In Thurston County, for example, the local bar association did not approve a set of forms for the use by members of the public. On the other hand, King County has adopted such forms. The necessary forms may also be obtained from stationery stores and in some books on the subject. Generally, the Clerk of the Court will give minimal assistance to the parties, explaining the mechanics of the divorce process but not verifying the accuracy of the legal papers prepared by the parties. 'Divorce kits' are available and have been used successfully in Washington courts, although they are not officially recognized as 'legal' by state and local authorities."

3. Correspondents from other states wrote courteous letters saying they could not give me definitive answers because their state law prohibited their doing so. But they were nice enough to send me the pertinent laws, manuals, and statutes of their states, taking the time to mark those provisions that contained answers to my questions.

4. Some states did not answer or wrote that they could not give me any help at all.

5. My state, Virginia, did itself proud: "I have completed part of the form and referred you to Xerox copies of relevant statutes." Trying to be thorough, I called the clerks of the courts in the two cities where I live and where my office is located. Both informed me that they would be willing to assist couples in

filling out the necessary papers for a no-fault divorce if the couples knew what they were doing.

6. From New York State I learned that in an uncontested divorce suit in Manhattan and the Bronx, the husband or wife is merely required to file papers with the Clerk of the Court, proving jurisdiction and other standard data to initiate the action. (But the Clerk of the Court is forbidden to give any advice or assistance in preparing the papers and completing the forms.) If the judge finds the papers in order, he can grant the divorce. Neither the husband nor the wife has to appear in court to end the marriage. If the papers are not in order, the judge will either hold a hearing or dismiss the suit.

So the answer to the question "Do I need a lawyer?" is, *Not necessarily. If your state gives you a constitutional right to represent yourself in court, you do not need a lawyer.*

Even if the Attorney General of your state says it cannot be done, if the state is one in which you have the right to represent yourself, my advice is to visit the Clerk of the Court in your city or county. His discretion is important. He may help you tremendously; but remember, he is not going to act as your attorney. He cannot practice law.

How do I choose a lawyer?

Do not choose a lawyer because he is a friend or because he has done legal work for you in another field of law. He may be a genius in real estate or insurance or corporation law, but not necessarily in divorce law.

What you need is a lawyer who specializes in divorce law and who has won a large percentage of divorce cases for men and women in your legal jurisdiction.

You are often with friends or business acquaintances or overhearing conversations of strangers who are going through divorce proceedings. They talk about it—in detail. LISTEN.

If the fees are identical, you would be foolish to engage a lawyer who wins only ten percent of his cases when you can obtain the services of another who wins 90 percent.

Unfortunately, the lawyer who is successful is usually expensive. The richer party can afford the lawyer who is going to make every effort to prolong the litigation. The poorer party, usually the woman, cannot afford a lawyer with that much expertise and is not going to be able to wait it out. Therefore, she is at a terrible disadvantage.

I have heard of Lawyer Referral Services. What are they?

If the Clerk of the Court cannot or will not cooperate, or if he is too incompetent to help you file papers correctly, the next least expensive method of obtaining a divorce may be through a Lawyer Referral Service.

The American Bar Association, sensitive to the fact that national polls place lawyers at the bottom of the totem pole of public trust, is now sponsoring a wonderful service in all states.

Based on the premise that the rich have their own lawyers and the poor are provided with free legal aid programs, but that millions of people of low to moderate means also need legal help, states, cities, and counties all over the country are forming Lawyer Referral Services, nonprofit programs aimed at making legal services inexpensive and easily available to the public.

For example, in Virginia any resident of the state who needs a lawyer can dial a toll-free number. You discuss your problem on the telephone and are first advised whether you require legal services. If you do not need a lawyer, you receive this information at no charge.

If you do need legal help, you are referred to a lawyer in your area who handles the kind of litigation called for. Or you may be referred to an organization or agency that can help.

For only $15 the attorney grants you a 30-minute consultation, during which he will try to answer every question that arises. (Fifteen dollars is the fee in Virginia. Other states have different fees, but all are very low.)

In 30 minutes, he should get enough information to advise you on your options. (He may say that you have no grounds for divorce.) If you decide to litigate, you can retain his services and negotiate a fee. But there is no obligation to retain him. He will even recommend another attorney if you so desire.

I mentioned the possibility of using your local Clerk of the Court to help you. The lawyer you are consulting can probably tell you whether it is worthwhile to go that route. Or he can tell you whether there are do-it-yourself kits in your state that are legally acceptable. He can advise you of their prices, and whether he thinks you are competent to use such a kit.

Are these lawyers any good?

From my experience I would say that they might be better than average. After all, they are performing this service because they want to help those who need help. They volunteer for the program. In Virginia, for example, 600 lawyers volunteered, including the attorney I use for most of my legal work. He is honest and competent. He gives the $15 client the same expertise that he gives me for a fee many times that amount.

This program is a landmark contribution to the American lawyer-client relationship.

(See chapter 29 for phone numbers to call in your state.)

If you visit a lawyer with some idea of what confronts you and if you read about your problems in this book before you use a Lawyer Referral Service, you will find the consultation much more enlightening then if you walk in without having done your homework. The more you know, the more you will learn from your attorney.

What about do-it-yourself kits and group services? How much do these do-it-yourself kits cost?

The price is low in some states and more than $135 in others. In New York State you can get a good kit for $39. These kits are legally acceptable in a growing number of states.

How do these kits work?

They include proper legal forms for you to fill out and written instructions for doing so. If the publisher is not a lawyer, he can give you no individual legal advice.

Is there any intermediate step between the do-it-yourself approach and hiring your own lawyer?

Some states now permit any bona fide organization to contract with a lawyer to provide group legal services at preset rates to bona fide members of the organization.

In New York, one of the most expensive divorce states, a group using this method has successfully established fees of $350 for a divorce and $225 for a separation. The group reasons that "there is no great skill required to write a decent separation agreement, nor does it take a legal genius, *once people are in agreement,* to draft a set of papers to go to court and effectuate a divorce."

Their spokesman continues, "What we do in my office is similar to what most doctors do in a group medical practice: we have highly trained paralegal secretaries, and we have questionnaires and forms. The paralegal secretaries work very closely with me and my staff on behalf of the union members. There is a 30-minute consultation. So no one is afraid to come into our offices in fear of being cheated.

"After obtaining a legal history from the client, the client's spouse is contacted and a meeting is arranged between both spouses and their lawyers.

"I have found that, given an hour or two of proper negotiation, the entire matter can be concluded. Most separation agreements are routine. There are certain provisions in a separation agreement which are not routine. They have to do with custody of children, visitation rights, alimony and support payments, life insurance, and medical benefits. These items are separately negotiated.

"Once the separation provisions are negotiated, and once we have discovered what the grounds of the divorce are, the information is fed to a paralegal assistant and secretary. In less than 30 minutes there is a complete set of divorce papers prepared, and a separation if that is also desired.

"The calendar in our local county is approximately ten to 15 days behind for an inquest. The matter is submitted for an inquest and our attorney appears with the client. It takes about 15 minutes of testimony on the stand. The judgment, having previously been prepared, is handed up to the judge sitting there, and he signs it, and the divorce is complete.

"It is a very simple process for middle-class people who do not have extensive assets."

I have quoted the statement at length because this approach is worth looking into if you belong to an organization and live in a state where such a plan can qualify. The obvious problems here lie in the broad scope of the services offered: "custody of children, visitation rights, alimony and support payments, life insurance, and medical benefits."

Before you decide on one of these alternatives to hiring your own lawyer, check on how satisfactory it has been by asking people who have used the given do-it-yourself kit or group services.

What will my divorce cost me?

There are several factors that lawyers consider in setting fees: (1) time expended, in and out of court; (2) results attained; and (3) the expertise of the lawyer, his special skills, and his prestige.

Lawyers who specialize in the divorce field may charge more for their time. One might charge $100 per hour, and another $50.

Most lawyers are reluctant to discuss fees with clients. Why, I don't know. But we are getting feedback today and, with all the public interest in consumerism, lawyers are becoming more concerned about whether or not they are having smooth relations with their clients.

The first time many clients use an attorney may be in a divorce action. They are scared to death, and rightly so. They don't know what it's going to cost. They have no idea how much time is going to be invested.

CASE IN POINT: Litigation for the husband results in his being ordered to pay $100 a week for child support, which will terminate when the child is 18. Suppose that's the extent of his liability. He pays no alimony. He will be shocked to be asked to pay a $500 fee, for which he had not been prepared. Lack of communication caused the problem.

When I first talked to New York attorneys who specialized in family law, I was horrified to hear that their fee for the simplest divorce was $2500. Some lawyers in my state, and others, gave me similar information. When I asked two well-known divorce lawyers why their fee was so high when a relatively easy divorce can be obtained in a very short time, they answered that they do not do things "hurriedly." They claimed that they had to study the situation carefully, and that it takes them months to complete the simplest divorce action because of their attention to detail and because of the New York court procedures.

Such lawyers are conning their clients. They remind me of architects who, on being commissioned to do a simple set of house plans which they could finish in one day, tell their clients that they have to do a "study" of the overall problem which will take weeks to accomplish. If the architect returned the completed plans to his client in a day or two with a bill of several thousand dollars, the client would rebel.

Likewise, if the lawyer makes his work look too simple to justify a very high fee, his client will rebel.

However, as a result of my appearances on television and radio talk shows, and as a result of newspaper publicity concerning my efforts to help the helpless, many dedicated lawyers and judges have voluntarily offered advice and encouragement in my endeavors.

CASE IN POINT: John P. O'Neill, attorney at law in Kew Gardens, New York, offered to help "in any way." He is so disillusioned by exorbitant fees and time-wasting tactics of divorce attorneys in general that he wrote an article for *New York* magazine in which he said that he handles the average uncontested divorce from beginning to end for just $350, and that divorce actions can be consummated in days or weeks rather than months or years. He shows in detail how little actual effort and expense is involved in drafting separation agreements and handling other legal matters necessary to obtain final divorce decrees. Here are some excerpts from the article:

"Most lawyers overcharge. Some charge as much as $5000 for a divorce. That's absurd. If two people can get together on a divorce (and they can, in at least half the cases), they should be able to find an attorney to handle it for $350."

"Let's face it—small lawyers have come on hard times. They need the work more than you need the divorce."

"Here's a young couple. No kids, no house, nothing. Married a couple of years. She split. Both wanted out. My costs were about $1.50 for the standard Blumberg forms that every lawyer in the state uses—and which a child could fill out—plus about $18 for typing. [On a case like this] I may never have to leave the office, and I can still clear about $300."

Even when the divorcing couple has property and children, a divorce need not be complicated: "Just because people have money is no reason to generate a lot of paperwork. No one in court reads it anyway."

"Even when the couple has kids, a house, and lots

of property, most separation agreements are practically standard, although lawyers charge hundreds for preparing them."

If there is such an agreement, O'Neill believes it is a mistake to stipulate in it an amount for child support. "It's too hard to change. If the couple leaves it up to the court to determine the amount of child support a man should pay, it's easy to change the support payments if circumstances change. But in a separation agreement, they are cast in bronze."

And O'Neill thinks courts are fairly reasonable in determining support payments. He cites the case of an amorous car-wash attendant. When he was dragged into court, he admitted fathering seven children by four different women. The judge fixed support payments at $3 per child per week.

"Any more, and the man would never have paid it. As it is, eventually over half the fathers default on support payments anyway."

How long should a divorce take? One lawyer told me, "About three months, once the papers are prepared. And that's because lawyers mess around with them. It can be a lot quicker. In my case, my wife managed it in three weeks. Of course, she knew how to go about it." She was a judge.

Who pays the lawyer's fees, husband or wife?

If the woman has no money, it is only fair that the man pay the lawyer's fees. Today, with many women working and earning more money than their husbands, in some states the court decides who pays the fees. The judge weighs the relative income and economic position of the parties. But in other states the husband must always pay the wife's legal fees.

What happens if the husband is legally supposed to pay the fee for the wife but does not do so?

A lawyer I know replied, "If I could collect the fee I would refund the sum of money I took from the other person, but I make it perfectly clear that I do not want to be a collection agency; I want to be paid for my services by the person who employed me."

The wife could ask the lawyer to give her a written agreement promising that, if she pays the fee to him in advance and her husband is later ordered by the court to pay her fee but doesn't, her lawyer will turn the bill over to another lawyer who specializes in collections.

(If a judgment is secured based on a court order, it can often be enforced like collection of a debt.)

I know too many women who complain bitterly that their husbands were ordered to pay the fee for them but failed to comply. They accuse their attorneys of making no effort to collect.

If the court orders the husband to make the payment and the husband refuses to do so, he is held under a contempt citation, and the judge can send him to jail.

However, the trend is to avoid putting the husband in jail for refusal to pay the wife's legal fees, alimony, and/or child support because the wife usually will be in worse shape if the husband is in jail. Therefore, pursuit of the husband for this failure is for her an exercise in futility.

If the husband must pay the wife's lawyer a definite fee, is that all the lawyer can charge her?

Definitely not. Many people are confused about this procedure. An attorney has the right to try to charge as much as he can. However, much too often the attorney neglects to explain the procedures in detail to his clients. The resulting shock is one of the reasons why lawyers have such a bad image.

Can my spouse and I have the same lawyer?

This is inadvisable unless there are no children and there is no estate.

Some lawyers will represent both parties in an uncontested divorce action. Others say "Never." They will not even draw up an agreement for either party waiving that party's rights in the action. If a battle ensues, dual representation could constitute conflict of interest and could be illegal.

What should the client learn from the lawyer during the first interview?

He should get some feeling whether the lawyer can communicate with him. After the lawyer has told him whether, based on the facts discussed, he has grounds for divorce, there should be a frank discussion of fees: What is the least it will cost if everything goes smoothly? How much could it cost if everything goes wrong? The client needs to know this range of fees. And, contrary to common belief, lawyers' fees are negotiable.

What does the lawyer have a right to expect from his client?

Complete honesty. There is nothing more embarrassing for a lawyer than to go into court basing his case on your facts, only to see the rug pulled from under him because of your lack of honesty.

2

During Your Divorce Action

Is it important who brings the action?

Years ago when women were looked upon as people who had no right to a job outside their home and to a life other than caring for children, it was socially unacceptable for a wife to be a defendant in a divorce action. It somehow reflected on character, and in "social circles" the wife was automatically considered the guilty party if she was the defendant. Possibly because of the double standard for the sexes, we already knew that men were committing more moral transgressions than women, therefore it was more socially acceptable for the husband to be the defendant.

The trend is changing. Now a divorce can often be obtained simply because the parties to the marriage have not lived together for a certain amount of time specified by state law. You can get a divorce without saying who left whom. And with no-fault divorce there is no reason to be concerned about who is the defendant and who "gets the divorce."

Do I lose rights in a no-fault divorce?

In general, you keep all your rights. But check the law of your state, to be on the safe side.

Today, no-fault divorces are awarded in many states if a couple has been separated for a year or more. The nonoffending party does not give up rights to alimony, support for the children, or general property dissolution. The suing party still has all the rights that would accrue to her should she bring the divorce action against the other person on grounds of desertion. The nonsuing party who has not committed any wrong is fully protected.

Can I obtain a divorce without my spouse knowing about it?

Such a divorce would be invalid and illegal, presuming that you know where the other person lives and that notice can be served. You would be stupid and ill advised to sneak off somewhere for a divorce. But see chapter 3.

Do I lose rights by not contesting a divorce?

Suppose a husband is awarded a divorce because his wife did not contest it. His only grounds were that he did not want the marriage anymore. Does the wife lose her right to alimony? She says that *she* had the legal grounds (adultery, desertion, assault) but did not sue for divorce.

And when she was served with the papers she never did anything: never answered, never waived anything. She just let it go. Even though she said she had legal grounds for divorce, no one was informed of them. She has lost all her rights to alimony unless the judge, in her absence, awarded her at least one dollar a year. This action keeps her foot in the door and gives her the right to come back and ask for more.

But, in general, if she does not show enough interest to appear to protect her rights, no judge is going to go out of his way to protect her. Only in an extreme case would an exception be made in her favor, namely, if she was unable to answer. (If she had personal notice—that is, if the papers had been handed to her in person—she could not come back for relief.) If no one informed her of the notice, she could come back and petition the court to file a late answer.

Can I move to another state during my divorce action?

You need not lose anything in your settlement by moving to another state before the divorce is final.

As long as you retain your lawyer in the place where the suit was filed and as long as the lawyer remains active in your case, continuing to represent you, you have every right to move to another state whether you are the suing or the sued party.

There are legitimate reasons for moving. For example, you might be the wife and, once the action is filed, find yourself financially unable to remain in your former domicile. So you go back home to live with your parents until the final decree is granted. Or you might leave the state fearing bodily harm. Or either party may work for a large national company and be transferred to another state.

However, if you run off to another state with another man or woman before the divorce becomes final, the settlement could be adversely affected if your actions are made known to the judge.

(See also chapter 12, "Out-of-State Garnishment.")

Can I give someone power of attorney to handle my divorce?

Power of attorney, with which you give someone else the legal right to act on your behalf, is permitted in many fields, but it cannot be used in the divorce action.

After a separation agreement has been drawn one party can give power of attorney to a third party to effectuate the agreement in regard to real estate transactions.

Can I date while I am waiting for my divorce?

If someone asks "How should I behave while my divorce action is pending?" he's often shopping for the answer he wants to hear. Some people go from lawyer to lawyer until they hear what they like.

Lawyers generally are going to tell you that during the divorce action it helps if you and your spouse behave civilly toward each other. This is not always easy. Sometimes there is bitter hatred. Couples with children and property are less likely to be amicable.

But what people most often want to know is if they can date. And certainly it would be reasonable to expect people to be able to date.

If there are children involved and one of the parents insists upon having custody of the children, lawyers would advise that parent to behave at home so that no one could say the children were being neglected or exposed to immoral conduct. The age of the children is a factor here.

Each situation has to be given individual consideration. But generally, people should try to be discreet in all their affairs. If they are not, they can be held answerable for the consequences of their conduct.

I'd like to add this piece of advice: Don't spy on your spouse. Try to understand that if the marriage is dead, the marriage is dead.

Can a divorce be amicable?

One never knows until after the final decree. Many separations start out amicably; both parties tell their friends that there will be no problem because they are reasonable. Then, when the negotiations begin, each becomes shocked at the other's attitudes, and the war is on.

So, even if you are both saying you are still friends, be cautious in what you say and do.

Do the news media have a right to expose details of my divorce case?

Suppose you live in a small community and you are going through a divorce, and somebody is admitting adultery, which is grounds for divorce in quite a few states. How embarrassing if it gets in the newspapers!

In a divorce action, how open to public exposure are the proceedings if the grounds are adultery? In other words, can the proceedings be held in private chambers, or does the battle have to be in court and does the press have the right to report every divorce action where adultery is the issue?

The answer varies from one state to another. In states where divorce is a completely open proceeding, everything is a matter of public record. Unless minors are involved, there is no statutory provision protecting anyone. An innocent person can be accused of adultery with a party in a divorce action, and the innocent person's name can appear in the papers. The newspapers and other media can say the person has been named as a third party in an adultery suit, and there is not much you can do about it.

How long till I get my divorce?

The divorce action lasts from the date of first filing suit until the final decree and possible appeal.

The law of each state is different. Assume that the grounds for divorce are satisfied and that both parties want the divorce with no reservations. In many states the petition for divorce can be filed, service accepted by the other party, waivers filed stating that neither party wants to appear in the case and that the parties want the order of divorce entered. The divorce commissioner hears the lawyers and files his report recommending the divorce. The final order is drawn up and presented to the judge. After he signs it, the divorce is final, except that in some states the order or decree may stay with the court for a number of days (typically, 21) during which the judge can amend his decree. When there is no divorce commissioner, the judge will hear the testimony.

So if everything goes on schedule, the entire divorce action can be completed in 30 days.

However, if there are children, money, and/or property involved, and the couple are fighting, the divorce action can stretch out for years and years.

3

One-Day Divorce (Mexico, Haiti, Dominican Republic); Nevada

You may have heard horrible things about Mexican divorces. There was that friend who had a Mexican divorce and was accused of bigamy because he remarried. So you wonder how legal are Mexican divorces and one-day Haitian and Dominican divorces.

This raises the question of full faith and credit by one nation toward another. Some years back, Mexican divorces were under attack on the grounds that only the party to the divorce suit who went to Mexico was represented in court. For this reason some courts in the U.S. held that Mexican divorces were not valid.

In order to overcome that objection, the nonappearing person can hire an attorney in Mexico and sign certain papers conferring jurisdiction on the Mexican court. Then, as most of our state courts have held, the person who signs those papers cannot later attack the decree in American courts. This seems to be the present state of the law—in general; and also for Haitian and Dominican divorces. I know many lawyers, doctors, and others who have gone to Haiti and the Dominican Republic for one-day divorces. So far, none of my acquaintances' divorces has been set aside.

But there are many ramifications with all these foreign divorces; legal advice is essential to find out whether these divorces are valid in your state.

Many people have gone to Nevada to get a divorce because they couldn't get it in their home state. Nevada's six-week residence requirement used to be very short compared to the other states. More and more states are now making residential, domicile and other requirements for divorce easier; therefore, you can usually secure a divorce in your home state more easily than by going to some other state and living there only for the statutory period after testifying under oath that you are going to make it your permanent home—a commitment you must make in Nevada and other states.

4

Counseling

The ethical lawyer will routinely advise his client to try reconciliation, unless he sees the marriage is irretrievably broken. This is what is meant by "counseling." Most ethical lawyers immediately question the prospective divorcée or divorcé about reconciliation. They ask: Are you certain that divorce is what you want? Have you talked it over calmly? Have you seen a marriage counselor? Do you realize the financial implications of divorce in your case? Do you realize what divorce is going to do to the children? Judges could act similarly if they had the time.

Several states *require* counseling to be offered to divorcing couples.

Suppose I live in such a state and counseling was not offered to me or my spouse by our lawyers or the judge. It would be difficult to have the divorce set aside because of this omission. I would have to come up with an exact definition of the word "counseling."

But neither a lawyer nor a judge has the obligation to act as a psychologist or a marriage counselor. A lawyer is a "counselor at law." He can claim that counseling is automatically part of his legal services. After all, he has advised you what to do.

Counseling is available to all who ask for it. But making it mandatory is unreasonable.

I have been married twice. I have been divorced twice. If I decide to marry again and the woman accepts, there is no power on earth that will force me to let some inexperienced college graduate come to my home to interview us. As long as I am willing to pay for my mistakes (financially, physically, and emotionally), I want those mistakes to be mine and not the result of counseling.

5

Hold-Harmless Agreements

Is it possible to write an ironclad agreement that prevents either party, after the divorce and final agreement, from taking further legal or other action against the former partner?

Before I consented to sign the proposed separation agreement with my first wife, I asked her lawyer and mine to draw up and approve a supplementary agreement in which I wanted it clearly stated that everything was finalized and that there would be no further harassment, embarrassment, or legal action against either party. It was drawn jointly by the two attorneys and notarized. Here is a copy of the agreement:

Agreement

THIS AGREEMENT is made this 3d day of March 1973, by and between DAVID I. LEVINE ("Mr. Levine") and BARBARA F. LEVINE ("Mrs. Levine").

WITNESSETH: That for and in consideration of Ten Dollars ($10.00), cash in hand paid, receipt acknowledged, and other good and valuable consideration, the parties hereto agree as follows:

1. If Barbara takes any legal action or other action directly or indirectly against David or any of his present family or staff, then Mrs. Levine agrees to hold Mr. Levine harmless from any

such action, and Mrs. Levine hereby agrees to pay any damages she should recover against Mr. Levine as a result of such action and to pay any and all expenses, including attorney's fees, which Mr. Levine incurs in defense of such action.

2. If David I. Levine takes any legal action or other action against Barbara, then Mr. Levine agrees to hold Mrs. Levine harmless from any such action, and Mr. Levine hereby agrees to pay any damages he should recover against Barbara, and to pay any and all expenses, including attorney's fees, which Mrs. Levine incurs in defense of such action.

WITNESS our hands and seals . . .

I lived up to this separation agreement, which was recorded in the four cities where we owned joint property.

We separated in early March, and in May, after the divorce, she refused to honor the agreement and engaged attorneys who threatened to sue me.

I was forced to hire an attorney in turn. He was supposed to be a genius of contracts and negotiations. When I showed him the agreement, he told me it was not worth the paper it was written on. I took him at his word, and there followed months of costly agonizing negotiations, in which I did not make proper use of the agreement.

Since then I have asked several attorneys if the agreement would have stood up in court. All said that, at least, it might. Most said that consideration, which is a necessary ingredient of every contract, was there, and that it would be recognized in court.

One attorney I asked for his professional reaction replied: "It means what it says. Had I represented either of you, and had the other threatened legal action, I would first have taken this agreement into court and asked for a ruling on its application to the matter at hand.

"But the agreement can apply only to what had happened as of the date of signing the agreement. Things unrelated to the subject matters covered in the separation agreement are not governed by it. Using an extreme example, if you slap her after the effective date of the agreement, you cannot go into court and claim immunity because the agreement relieved you of liability."

If additional legal or other action is taken against me, I shall engage an attorney who will guarantee to present the agreement to the proper court or jurisdiction. Then I can give a better answer on the validity of legal agreements.

But I fervently hope that the agreement never has to be tested. I'd rather not have the action and not know the answer.

6

Tricks Lawyers Play

Why do many husbands and wives in divorce actions end up hating their attorneys more than they hate their spouses?

Part of the answer is that no one is ever satisfied with the results of a divorce. Divorce does not mean that you will never have no further relationship with your ex-spouse. It does not mean you are never going to have another mutual problem. So people often become angry because they are still having problems.

The problems are usually not the lawyer's fault. They are the same problems that caused the dissolution of the marriage, indicating that divorce may indeed be desirable. But the problems are connected with the lawyer's role. So the client blames his attorney although the fault is his own and the lawyer is just doing his duty.

(Some of it is game playing; people like to "involve" their attorneys, and there are attorneys who are foolish enough to let themselves be drawn into that trap.)

But there are lawyers that play unethical tricks—legal and illegal ones—on unsuspecting husbands and wives.

Without going too deeply into the question of ethics, let's talk about some of these tricks so that we can be more alert when we encounter them and avoid some of the frustration they can cause.

Delaying tactics

The most irritating thing lawyers do to their clients is to stretch out cases deliberately, or accidentally, or through inattention. A man or woman in a divorce action is usually upset anyway, and at least one party to the divorce is anxious to end it. Uncertainty and indecision can cause nervous breakdowns or can force one party to give in through sheer desperation.

In particular, when there is money involved, many lawyers will draw the case out forever, demanding unnecessary depositions, asking for details that have no real bearing on the case. This is done for the purpose of building up fees.

There are dozens of ways cases can be delayed. Your lawyer may tell you he cannot get the other lawyer to answer his phone calls or letters. He may tell you that he cannot get dates set for hearings when actually he can. He may go on demanding additional papers from you that he knows are difficult for you to produce, even though he knows they are irrelevant.

In many law firms one member is in the state legislature. If that firm's strategy is to wear down the other client, the firm lets the legislator be the lawyer of record. That gives the lawyer "legislative immunity." This "poor" lawyer cannot be in two places at the same time, and since in the eyes of the court the state's business is more important than the business of some poor housewife, we will all just have to wait until the end of the legislative session.

It doesn't even have to be a lawyer. All a law firm has to do is contact any person in the legislature who could appear as a witness and get the court to postpone the case because that person is needed in the state capital. The judge does not have to be convinced of the relevance of that witness's testimony.

Such tactics are, of course, not limited to divorce actions.

CASE IN POINT: I had a million-dollar-plus case against a builder, and the judge permitted the other side to delay the trial again and again, nearly giving the defendant enough time to bankrupt the corporation I was suing. The final straw came when the case was actually in court and I had expert witnesses and lawyers fly in from all over the country. The judge announced, like an innocent babe, that the case had to be postponed because an architect called by our opponents as a witness was in legislative session. The architect's testimony could have had no decisive bearing on the case.

Lack of communication

Another thing that turns people against their lawyers is lack of communication. It is very frustrating not to get an answer from your attorney. It is even worse to get an evasive, confusing, or incorrect answer.

Lawyers seldom voluntarily keep clients abreast of what is going on. I paid an attorney thousands of dollars, but he never routinely sent me copies of the pleadings or correspondence. Even when he knew I was aware that he had a hearing on a matter of mine, he never called me to report. And why don't lawyers want their clients to be with them when they meet with opposing attorneys or when they are in the judge's chambers?

There are several possible answers. Some clients are unreasonably emotional and could, in the lawyer's honest opinion, make matters worse. But some lawyers do not want their clients to realize how incompetent they are and how poorly they represent them. It is much easier for the lawyer to report back to the client that the opposing attorney was unreasonable or that the judge was stupid or tough.

It is seldom that the client does not know the details of his affairs better than his lawyer knows them. After all, the poor client has only one or two things on his mind during the divorce action. The lawyer may have hundreds of other clients. So, after the passage of weeks or months or even years, the lawyer forgets a good deal about the case—at his client's expense.

An attorney I know told me the following:

"The greatest shortcoming we lawyers have is our failure to communicate with our clients about what is going on in the case. Sometimes we are hard to reach.

"Too often we do not take the client into our confidence. We go back into the judge's chamber without the client, and we settle the case, and then come out and tell the client what the judge did and what we did and said. But the client was not present at the hearing. He cannot be certain that our account of the events is accurate.

"As businessmen and human beings we should want our clients to know everything that is happening. We should want them to be satisfied with the services that are provided. They are not going to be satisfied if they get a bill for $200 or $300 or $500 and have no idea what we have done for them and how we did it.

"So the trend today is to have the client present as often as feasible, make him aware of the status of his case, and send him copies of all papers and letters written, so that he has an appreciation of everything that is done for him."

When I have a conference with my attorney, I like to take two or three of my associates along with me so that, after the conference, we can compare notes and see if we agree on what the attorney said and what he advised. Most lawyers use confusing terminology, so you are justified in taking someone along with you to help you understand what happens.

Most lawyers with whom I have dealt do not like this. They say that it cancels out the confidentiality factor in the lawyer-client relationship. But the real reason why they don't like it is different: They make so many mistakes that they do not want you to have witnesses to their inattention, their stupidity, or their carelessness.

Conflicting answers

If you ask three lawyers the same question about your divorce action, you will get three different answers.

(But keep in mind that you may have varied the facts or wording in asking your questions. Also, in many cases there are no definitive answers.)

By the same token, one lawyer never likes another lawyer's contract. He will always find something wrong with a contract that was not drawn by himself. And you can ask the same lawyer the same question about a point of law on two occasions, and, often, you will receive two different answers.

Promise of success

A lawyer who tells you that you cannot lose your case is misleading you. Any case can be won or lost. Be suspicious of a lawyer who guarantees success.

On the other hand, be suspicious of a lawyer who tells you that the case is just about impossible to win, but that he will do his best.

Then there are lawyers who realize the client has no grounds for a suit but take the case anyway. The temptation may be greater if the possible fees are substantial.

Judge shopping

Some lawyers tell you they will try to choose or veto a specific judge. Such a maneuver may seem to be in your favor. But beware: the strategy here is to condition you to expect nothing so that you will appreciate anything you win.

An attorney usually does not choose the judge but must accept the one who appears on the calendar; but a smart lawyer who knows the ins and outs of court procedures in his area can legitimately get the case into the court he feels may be most favorably disposed toward his type of courtroom tactics.

In October 1976 I appeared on a television talk show in New York City and made the preceding statement. A prominent lawyer on the program disputed my contention with "Come on, Mr. Levine, you are generalizing. If you are going to make such accusations, you are going to have to give me names. I appear in court today, and tomorrow I can't even remember the name of the judge who heard the case."

CASE IN POINT: From the (Norfolk) *Virginian Pilot,* March 3, 1977: "A new docket system, under which a circuit court judge decides which judge will try the case the day before it is scheduled was instituted Wednesday in Norfolk Court by Chief Judge Morris B. Gutterman.

"The change will tend to eliminate 'judge shopping' by lawyers seeking the best deal for their clients.

"Lawyers, in collaboration with the commonwealth's attorney's office, will be able to set the date of trial but will be unable, *as they did in the past,* to pick a courtroom, which was tantamount to selecting a judge."

Vetoing a specific judge is never easy. You need valid reasons. It's a rare judge who will readily accept your reasoning, and you are always faced with the risk of being cited for contempt of court if the judge feels offended. To appeal a contempt citation is hardly worth the time and effort. You are playing ball on the judge's home field, and he makes all the rules.

Misplaced documents

It is hard to believe how many times lawyers misplace important documents, or lose them altogether.

Of course it is you, the client, who suffer.

Bribing of witnesses

Lawyers can hurt clients by bribing witnesses.

If a lawyer bribes somebody to testify to things that aren't true, he can be punished by being disbarred. But what counts most is that it hurts you, the client.

Request for a piece of the action

Many lawyers today want "a piece of the action" when a client comes to them for legal advice about new business ventures—often in the wake of a divorce. Is this attitude advantageous to the client?

On the face of it, it would seem to be, the lawyer gives better service to a client in whose business he has an interest. But, realistically, avoid any lawyer who takes "a piece of the action." The best lawyers are those who practice *law*. The minute a lawyer gets into a business venture (or into politics), his own interests will inevitably be given precedence over the client's. If the business venture sours, the lawyer is going to spend valuable time worrying about his problems rather than yours. A fine attorney goes to sleep mapping out strategy for winning his clients' cases. One with his fingers in many personal pies will not spend much time worrying about your problems.

Breach of confidentiality

Your attorney should protect your confidence, and not discuss your affairs with outsiders. You have the right to feel that whatever you tell your lawyer will remain with him and will not be discussed with others without your permission.

If a social worker is drawn into a case to do a social history, your attorney may ask you to sign something analogous to a medical release allowing him to reveal certain information to the social worker. Very often social workers are brought into write reports if children are involved. If the social worker is going to contribute anything of value to the case, information is needed that can be obtained only from the client and from the lawyer.

But if your attorney discusses your case with outsiders without your permission, you can take action against him. Every bar association has a committee on ethics. It is proper for you, under oath, to set forth the factual situation and make a complaint which will be investigated. Disciplinary action may be instituted. The lawyer is entitled to a hearing at which you and all the witnesses may appear before a committee, and ultimately before judges. In most jurisdictions there is a panel of judges to try the case, much like the way a criminal case is tried. The charge is very serious: a lawyer can be disbarred for betraying the confidence of a client.

Malpractice

If the committee on ethics pronounces a lawyer guilty of malpractice in a divorce action, the client may be entitled to financial compensation.

Malpractice cases against lawyers have become become much more common. If the lawyer makes a mistake as the result of negligence, he is liable to a potential malpractice claim as long as the client can show damages resulting from the negligence. Divorce is a ripe area for malpractice suits because of the important financial settlements often involved.

An important area where clients can suffer substantial loss is taxes. Unfortunately, many lawyers have not kept themselves informed of the basic tax aspects of divorce.

PART TWO

The Divorce Terms

7

Alimony

The three things that concern couples the most in a divorce action are, in order of importance:

1. Alimony (spousal support).
2. Custody of children and child support.
3. Decision on who gets the home and personal property.

Each of these will be discussed in detail from the legal and tax standpoints in this and the following chapters.

Alimony is money that one spouse pays the other for support and maintenance, either by agreement of the parties or because it has been forced on one party. It is paid as a lump sum, as periodic payments, or both.

Almost everyone has some idea of what alimony is. But several states no longer use the term "alimony." Some call it support or support and maintenance. Calling it spousal support seems to be the trend. But they all mean the same thing. So do not be frightened or relieved if you hear there is no longer alimony in your state but only "spousal support."

There is good reason why other terms are replacing "alimony." Most laymen, lawyers, and judges feel that alimony must cease upon remarriage. (It does, in the eyes of the Internal Revenue Service.) If support payments for the spouse are designated "alimony," further payments after remarriage are very unlikely.

My advice is to be sure that the support payments are never called "alimony" alone. If your state still uses the term "alimony," then use the extended term "alimony and/or spousal support." This protects the paying party in that he will enjoy a tax deduction until his former wife remarries. It protects the receiving party in that she will continue to receive spousal support for a specified period of time even after remarriage because the "alimony" converts into a contractual obligation. So the addition of a few words in your separation agreement may avoid confusion and heartache.

The answers to the following questions have been kept general. No two states have identical divorce laws. But if you study these questions and answers as guidelines, you will have a better understanding of how legal and tax matters are handled. I cannot emphasize too strongly that the lawyer and the judge are as important as the law itself.

Q: I have heard of "separate maintenance." What kind of alimony is that?

A: Separate maintenance is awarded pending a final divorce decree, or an action for annulment, or a separate action for alimony without divorce. It does not have any necessary relationship to the amount of alimony that will be awarded in the final decree; it is considered a reasonable amount of money, payable monthly as a rule, to enable the spouse to survive financially until the final settlement.

You can sue for separate maintenance while living apart without seeking divorce or legal separation.

Q: If we are not divorced and the payment is called separate maintenance, is it still alimony?

A: Yes. There are three requirements for alimony: (1) it must be in writing; (2) it must be in a written separation agreement, a decree of divorce, or a decree of support; (3) the payments must be periodic. They are deductible by the husband, and the wife has to treat them as income for tax purposes.

Q: Is the husband obligated to maintain the wife in the style of living to which she was accustomed?

A: It is not that simple. Her accustomed style of living is taken into consideration, but many other factors must be considered:

1. The parties' earning capacities, obligations, needs, and financial resources.

2. Their education and training, and their abilities and opportunities to secure further education and training.

3. The standard of living established during the marriage.

4. The duration of the marriage.

5. Age and physical and mental condition of the parties.

However, there may be grounds for a spouse not to have to pay permanent support and maintenance. If adultery is established, the offending spouse may not be awarded alimony at all, and will almost certainly be awarded much less alimony, regardless of the standard of living enjoyed during marriage. The discretion of the court prevails.

CASE IN POINT: A prestigious professional has income of $120,000 a year. He and his wife have three children. The judge awards the wife alimony and child support of only $1500 per month, after examining the records learning that the husband has made some bad investments and is in financial difficulty. The judge, thus, gives more weight to the financial condition of the husband than to the style of living to which the wife was accustomed.

In an almost identical case another judge said, "The devil with the debts. Your wife and children come first. You are going to pay her $2200 per month."

Q: Can a judge's ruling on alimony be appealed to a higher court?

A: You can try to appeal any judge's ruling, but you should be aware of the fact that it is rare for decisions of lower courts to be overruled. The presumption of the higher court is that the lower-court judge, with his firsthand knowledge of parties at law, is better able to determine who is telling the truth and what the facts in the case are. Normally, a lower-court decision is overruled only on points of law, rather than fact.

Appeals are expensive. If you are stubborn and are willing to spend the money for an appeal simply to delay the final outcome, your attorney may proceed even though he has informed you that your chances are slim or nil. But unless your lawyer can convince you, with citations from prevailing legal cases, that the lower court erred, it is better not to waste your time and money, your energy and emotions, on a hopeless cause.

Q: Is there any other way to change a divorce decree?

A: Yes. Asking for an appeal should not be confused with asking for modification. You can go back to the same court that granted the divorce decree and plead that, due to change in circumstances, alimony should be increased or decreased. A review will be granted.

CASE IN POINT (MODIFICATION): The wife proves that the husband's income has doubled since alimony was first awarded and she shows an inflationary factor of 20 percent. She asks for more money, and will probably have the decree modified giving her more, though not necessarily as much as she asks for.

CASE IN POINT (APPEAL): In a noncommunity property state the judge awarded the family home to the wife in the same decree in which he granted the divorce. The husband appealed on the grounds that the judge made a mistake in law, since that state, does not permit property awards in divorce actions, only alimony, custody, and child support. The higher court overruled the judge's decree.

Q: Does alimony automatically stop if the party receiving it remarries?

A: Recently, several states have gone in opposite directions. In some states, even if the husband proves that his ex-wife is living with another man, the court will not modify or revoke alimony. In other states, in the absence of a separation agreement stating that the husband will pay the wife alimony for a certain period of time even if she remarries, alimony does not have to be paid from the date of the remarriage.

In my state, Virginia, the state legislature passed a law that permits the husband to stop paying alimony to the ex-wife on her remarriage, even if the husband and wife have agreed in their separation agreement that alimony payments will continue for a specified number of years.

This new Virginia law cannot stop the husband from voluntarily continuing to pay his ex-wife. But to stop making payments he only has to go back into court and quote the new statute. This is unfair to the wife who has granted her husband a divorce in good faith, relying on his written contract to pay her alimony for a given number of years regardless of remarriage.

It is also unfair because the IRS will not allow an alimony deduction to the husband for voluntary payments after her remarriage, and he will therefore be less inclined to live up to his contract. If he does make the payments, the IRS may even impose a gift tax on them.

Q: How does a no-fault situation affect alimony?

A: Alimony is discretionary in no-fault divorces, depending on the situation. It is not mandatory.

Q: If a bank account is in only one name, can the other spouse get a share of it upon divorce?

A: She can get it in community property states if the account was opened after the marriage, but not in other states.

Q: If the husband works for the government, can his pay be garnisheed?

A: It can now. Child support and alimony are two of the few things for which you can garnishee a federal employee under federal law. Your local juvenile and domestic court will handle this for you.

Q: Every three months I am brought into family court with my ex-wife. Every time the judge refuses her request for additional alimony and/or child support. Why do I have to keep paying the lawyer's fee in the family court?

A: If you are referring to *your* lawyer's fee, the remedy is simple. You know the procedure. You know your own affairs as well as your lawyer does. So next time go without a lawyer, and you will not have to pay that fee. If you are referring to *her* lawyer's fee—every time a husband and a wife go to court for an increase, in most states it is the husband who has to pay his *and* her lawyer, at the discretion of the court.

Q: If a wife lives in one state with her husband and leaves him and moves to another state, is the husband obligated to pay alimony?

A: The question is too general. If she leaves him and moves to another state, he can file a suit against her for desertion.

If she felt that she had to get away from him because she was in mortal fear of what he might do to her (physically or mentally) she could sue him for "constructive desertion," provided she lives in a state where that is a ground for divorce.

If she is in a state where there is a juvenile or domestic relations court, he can be served with notice under the reciprocity statutes in the state where he now lives. After she files a nonsupport petition, a hearing will be arranged in her state on what he earns. The courts can order him to provide her and the children with support, even though she is in another state.

The only way he can stop paying her support is to file a suit for desertion in her state. That will stop her unless she comes back and fights it, trying to prove that she did not desert him.

Q: Can I place a limit on medical and dental payments? Suppose she has several teeth capped for $1000 or has surgery performed. Suppose she wants a face-lift.

A: You can and should try to set a limit. Your payments usually cover costs like hospitalization premiums, but not expenses in excess of payments made by the health insurance company in comformity with the policy on which you paid premiums (such as Blue Cross/Blue Shield).

Q: Can I agree to pay medical premiums until remarriage or for a specific amount of time?

A: Time and money limits should be spelled out in the agreement in order to avoid misunderstanding every time a new crisis develops.

Q: If I make less than $15,000 per year and I have to pay alimony, do I pay on each dollar? In other words, is the alimony payment a predetermined percentage of the $15,000?

A: There is much misunderstanding about this. At present, there are no general guidelines for alimony. So the answer is no.

Q: If my ex-wife starts working, do I still have to pay alimony and/or child support?

A: It is at the discretion of the judge, if there was no separation agreement. When husband and wife are both working, the courts can order both to support the children. At any rate, if you agreed in the separation agreement to pay her without stipulating that your payments would be reduced or stopped if she goes to work, you have to continue paying her. The payments can be stopped only by her death or remarriage.

CASE IN POINT: It was his idea to have a separation agreement. She now has a good income. Had it covered her present employment, her alimony or child support could have been reduced. If there was no separation agreement, he could go to court and ask for reduction of alimony and/or child support.

CASE IN POINT: An executive working for a national magazine gave me a copy of the separation agreement he had committed himself to sign. He was worried about a provision that he would continue to pay the same alimony unless she earned in excess of $13,000 per year. It did not stipulate how much less he was to pay per dollar she earned over $13,000. (Still, in this case the wife would be well advised to keep her income under $13,000. Each $1000 per year earned might cost her several times that much in lost alimony.)

Q: Does a woman necessarily have a claim on her husband's pension?

A: No. But the question is incomplete. We

should also ask, "If the husband's sole source of income is his pension, can the court order him to provide support for his former spouse?" Here the answer is yes.

Q: If I live with a man and he is supporting me, will I lose my alimony?

A: If a woman is divorced and she is living with another man, a judge will seldom say he will stop her from receiving alimony. It is at the discretion of the judge. But the situation is good leverage for the husband. If she lives with a man during the period from the filing to the final decree of divorce and the court learns of it, it will have a great effect on what the spouse is awarded, if anything.

Q: What is an alimony trust?

A: The alimony is put in a third party's name. The third party takes care of the proceeds. (For more details, see chapter 21.)

Q: If either party foolishly and impetuously gives the spouse everything, can he or she later go back for a review and relief?

A: Yes. But the circumstances must be very persuasive. (Anyone can bring suit, even frivolously. It is costly, and a reputable attorney will advise the client not to take such actions. But there is almost always some lawyer who, for money, will represent any client in any action. Thousands of legal actions every year are motivated only by hate, jealousy, and pique.)

Q: My wife and I are not really angry at each other. We have been living together for many years and trust each other and I say, "Look, without going to the expense of having agreements written by lawyers, why don't I just promise to give you a certain amount of money a month?" If we agree to that, am I entitled to a tax deduction?

A: No. The agreement must be in writing, or the payments will not be deductible to you nor are they income to her. They are not alimony.

Q: Suppose I agree to give her a principal alimony sum of $90,000, paying $10,000 a year for nine years. Is this deductible to me as an expense?

A: No, because the time period is only nine years. Alimony must meet the IRS requirements that the principal sum has to be payable for a period of ten years or more.

Q: If I cannot get a tax deduction on what I pay her, does she have to pay income tax on it?

A: No. But if you agree, in writing, to pay her a fixed amount for a period of 15 years, that is alimony. You can deduct it as an expense and it is taxable to her as income.

Q: Suppose I agree to pay her for 15 years and she dies after 12 years. Will I still have to pay somebody for another three years?

A: Yes, you will have to pay her estate for three years.

Q: Suppose I die three years before my agreed-upon alimony payments expire. Does my estate have to pay her or her estate for another three years?

A: Yes, your estate will still have to pay, because this is a contractual liability.

Q: Are lump-sum settlement payments advisable?"

A: For the receiving party, very much so. With a lump-sum payment there is no income tax liability for the receiving party. Also there are no nagging worries about whether alimony will ever be paid.

CASE IN POINT: A woman has the choice of taking $6000 per year for ten years or a $50,000 lump-sum settlement. If she chooses the $6000 for ten years she will have to pay state and federal income taxes on it. Because she earns additional income, her taxes on the $6000 alimony are quite high. (If she earns $6000 salary plus her $6000 alimony and is single, her federal income tax, after standard deduction, will be over $2,000.) However, if she chooses the $50,000 lump-sum settlement, she can invest it in ten-year high-interest-rate bonds (ten percent) with safe and reputable companies: she will receive $5000 interest for each of the ten years and have the $50,000 intact at the end of the period.

Q: Do we have the right to agree on how much alimony and how long I pay her, without interference from the judge?

A: You have the right to agree to any form of alimony settlement you wish. The tax question remains whether the husband can deduct alimony payments or take them out of his income, and whether they are counted as income to his spouse.

Q: Must alimony be free and clear? For example, if I agree to give her $1000 a month alimony, and in return she agrees to give up a 50 percent interest in a piece of property that we own together, is this pure alimony?

A: No. It would not be a deductible expense to you and would not be taxable income to her. You cannot combine a cash payment with a property settlement. Alimony has to stand on its own to qualify.

Q: Suppose she needs a degree in order to qualify for a higher-paying job, and I agree to pay for her education. She may choose to attend a beauty parlor school to learn to be an operator or to attend a university to get a Ph.D. If I pay her school expenses, is that alimony?

A: Yes, but every detail has to be spelled out clearly in your separation agreement.

Q: What about the husband's payment of the wife's income taxes? Part of an agreement is often that he pays her taxes. How long is he expected to pay them? Are his payments deductible like alimony?

A: The length of time and the terms are a matter on which the two parties must agree. But it is alimony. You may agree to pay the tax on the first $6000 she earns each year for five years after the divorce. (This avoids the possibility of paying a small amount of taxes at first, then learning that she has secured a high-paying job which will force you to pay more than you anticipated.) Your separation agreement should specify the number of years, and limit the amount of income on which you will pay taxes.

Q: What about payment of life-insurance premiums in relationship to alimony? Are they deductible as alimony?

A: Yes—as long as she, not he, owns the policy. Usually the wife will appreciate it if the husband continues to pay the premiums. (For more details, see chapter 16.)

Q: What about mortgage payments on the home or apartment? Let's assume the man leaves the woman in the home they jointly own. The home is still in both their names, and in their separation agreement he agrees to continue paying mortgage payments, interest, and real estate taxes on the home. Is that alimony?

A: The mortgage payments on a jointly owned home are not alimony, and he cannot deduct them. They do not meet the IRS requirements. But he will be allowed deductions for the interest and real estate taxes he pays.

Q: Suppose the home is in her name only. Are mortgage payments, interest, and real estate taxes alimony?

A: Yes. They are deductible by him and taxable as income to her.

Q: Are legal fees in a divorce action deductible?

A: Ordinarily, no. But try to get your lawyer to separate fees attributable to legal action from those involved in the property settlement. You may be allowed a deduction for fees charged for the property settlement.

8

Child Support, Custody, and Visitation Rights

Q: Can the wife collect alimony and child support if the husband moves to another state?

A: Under the Uniform Reciprocal and Support Act, the wife can go to the juvenile and domestic relations court in her city, which will take her deposition. She gives affidavits and outlines her support needs, and gets an order from the court that she has a need of X dollars per week, or month, to be contributed by the husband. She has to know where the husband is to do this.

Q: Can the wife collect alimony and child support if the husband skips to another country, like Canada? Which countries are best for skipping?

A: Reciprocity with a foreign country does not work as it does between the states of the U.S.A. You would have to locate the husband in Canada and go there, which can be expensive. The time and effort would seem to be justified only if the husband is worth a fortune.

Q: What can you do if your husband has stopped making child-support payments and you don't know his whereabouts?

A: Your first step should be to contact the Bureau of Support Enforcement in your locality. Ask your local Social Services Bureau (or Welfare Department) or the office of the commonwealth or district attorney for the address.

In Virginia, for example, your city's Bureau of Support Enforcement will ask you to come in and fill out a form providing general information on your husband: his address, last place of employment known to you, name and address of his nearest relatives, etc. The bureau sends the information to the Parent Location Service in Richmond, which contacts any agency or individual who may know of your husband's whereabouts within the state, including other state agencies such as the Division of Motor Vehicles.

If in-state research yields no results, the Parent Location Service will contact the National Parent Location Service in Washington, D.C., which will begin a nationwide search for your husband.

All this entire process usually takes three to six weeks.

Then the local court sends the depositions and the order of the Virginia court to the appropriate juvenile and domestic relations court in the state where the husband now lives. He will be summoned, and a hearing will be conducted. The judge will honor the order. (The husband's only defense would be if there was another order entered in either state.)

Q: Is there a juvenile court in every state?

A: Yes, though perhaps not by that name.

Q: What happens if the parties live in different states and each has a different court order?

A: Where there is conflict, the children come first. The court in the state where the children reside has jurisdiction over support.

Q: Are there general guidelines for child support?

A: Child support depends on the circumstances of the parties, especially on which spouse has income. Increasingly today, either spouse can be charged with liability. If child support cannot be agreed on by husband and wife, you can forget the guidelines, because the judge is going to decide what in his opinion is reasonable. Both spouses are likely to be dissatisfied.

Q: Does the court govern all matters pertaining to the children? Do the parents have any say?

A: The parents can agree on custody and support of the children and visitation rights; but their agreement is subject to review by the court. As long as there is nothing in the agreement detrimental to the children's well-being, the court will approve the agreement.

Q: Does the court review its ruling on children periodically even if no one protests?

A: No. The court will review its ruling only if a review is requested.

Q: If the agreement stipulates that my husband will support the children until they are 21, can new laws that make them adults at 18 affect the agreement? Will my ex-husband still have to support them until they are 21?

A: Yes, but if the age is not spelled out, 18 will prevail, unfair as it may sound.

Note that if the children are totally disabled, particularly if they go to a state institution, the parents are obligated to support them for life. (On the other hand, children have to take care of parents who are disabled.)

In general, if your separation agreement is valid, your former spouse is legally obliged to live up to it. That is why I strongly recommend that the agreement be incorporated into the final divorce decree. It makes it easier for the judge to have all the paperwork in one file and leaves no room for arguing about the validity of the agreement.

Q: I am divorced and have two children in my legal custody. My 14-year-old daughter has chosen to live with her father. I have not signed papers giving him custody. Is he entitled to return of the money he gives me toward her support?

A: No. But if he goes to court and the judge amends his order in view of her living with him, giving custody to him, the judge can adjust child support at his discretion.

Q: Can a premarital agreement permit me to

waive rights to alimony and child support if the proposed marriage ends in divorce?

A: You can waive alimony. You can never waive child support.

Q: Are there any guidelines or is there anything a lawyer can do about visitation rights?

A: Most lawyers proceed on the basis that the more specific the visitation rights are—and let's hope those rights are in writing—the better off you are. People like to nitpick. (An example: A man was 15 minutes late picking up his children. The ex-wife, who had custody, would not open the door or had left with the children before he arrived. Naturally, it is the children who are the victims of such actions.)

Q: The final decree does not mention what happens if the mother, who has custody leaves the state. If she moves and visitation is impractical for geographical reasons, can the father withhold alimony and/or child support?

A: No. But he can request the court to let him have the children during the summer or extended holidays. If he's granted the request, the order should be incorporated in the decree.

Q: Can you get protection from harassment by the other party after the divorce?

A: You can have an order entered. But since we are dealing with human beings, there can always be harassment in one form or another, no matter what judges say or do.

Q: Is there any legal protection against a parent who uses "psychological warfare" to alienate the children from the other parent?

A: Lawyers can do very little about it. But a malicious campaign by one parent against the other often backfires. As the children grow older, they mature and begin to think for themselves.

Children have few rights in our society. They bear the brunt of adult foolishness. But here they can play the role of judge and jury. Society cannot legislate love and affection, which have to be earned.

9

Adoption

Q: If you want to adopt your spouse's children, is it a federal matter or does each state have different laws?

A: Each state has its own laws.

Q: If I marry a woman and want to adopt her children, and the father is alive, do I have to get his consent?

A: Yes.

Q: Suppose I can't find the father of my spouse's children. He has disappeared and he is not paying alimony. Can anything be done to go ahead with adoption?

A: If he has disappeared and it is believed that he is out of the country or dead, a judge, after public notice has been given of the intended adoption, can extinguish the rights of the absent parent. But only in extreme circumstances will a court allow a person's parental rights to be extinguished by adoption without his consent.

Q: What happens to my adopted children if their mother and I get a divorce?

A: They are still yours. There is no way you can "unadopt" them unless she marries someone else who agrees to adopt them. Therefore I'd recommend you live a long time with a spouse and her children before you offer to adopt them. You must be certain that you are willing to become their legal parent for the rest of your life.

But on the other hand, in the introduction to this book I recommended you enter a new relationship with warmth and enthusiasm. Suppose that in dating your future bride you have learned to love her children and feel that they love you. Nothing could be more touching and help cement the marital relationship more than your show of faith and confidence in agreeing to adopt her children.

There is a mandatory waiting period before adoption. It can also be a testing period. If, before the final papers are executed, the whole relationship blows up, you do not have to go through with the adoption proceedings.

10

House and Apartment

The following questions and answers do not apply to community property states. (See chapter 17.)

Let's look at the types of ownership in most non-community property states.

1. *Tenants by the entirety with right of survivorship:* This is the best way for a married couple to take title to a home unless they are very wealthy and do not need nor want the protection this affords. A couple must be married to take title as tenants by the entirety. The advantage is that if one spouse incurs a debt, the creditor cannot move against the home for nonpayment; only if both husband and wife sign for an indebtedness can the creditor so move. This is why many creditors who make large sales on credit or make loans to a married couple ask them both to sign for the indebtedness. Most lawyers will advise a couple buying a home for the first time to take title as tenants by the entirety. But this manner of taking title is not used in many states today. Right of survivorship guarantees that if either spouse dies, the other spouse receives the whole home.

2. If the couple do not want all of the home to belong to the surviving spouse, they can buy the home as *tenants in common.* Then if one tenant in common dies, half the value of the home goes to the remain-

ing spouse and the other half into the estate of the deceased.

3. If a married couple own their home as tenants by the entirety and are later divorced, ownership is automatically converted to tenants in common, where she gets her half if he dies, and the other half goes to his estate.

4. Some states have *dower rights* This means the husband, even if he has the home in his name only, cannot sell it without getting her signature on the deed of conveyance. Dower rights exist only during marriage. A divorce destroys the right of a wife to dower.

5. An unmarried couple can take title to a home as *joint tenants with right of survivorship.* Right of survivorship guarantees that if either owner dies the other owner receives the whole home; but neither joint tenant is protected against creditors.

Q: If my husband owned the house in his name before we were married, and never transferred the title to me, am I entitled by law to any part of it upon divorce?

A: No.

Q: Suppose I helped make the payments on a home that is in my husband's name only. Am I entitled to any part of it when we get divorced?

A: No—not even if you made all the payments. But you might have other claims against him. You might try showing your canceled checks to the judge, claiming that you made a loan or an advance and so are entitled to a refund.

Q: What share does each spouse own if the couple purchases the house jointly after marriage? If a house is bought by either spouse before marriage and later put in their names jointly, is it treated as belonging 50 percent to each spouse?

A: Half; yes.

Q: I have two young children and I am still legally married. When we were buying a house I did not think in terms of divorce. I was very naive. As a result the house is in my husband's name only. My husband says he will put in writing that when he sells the house he will give me 50 percent of the proceeds. How shall I handle this?

A: You are right, you were very naive. Try to get him to deed a 50 percent interest in the house to you right now, while he is in a generous mood.

If you cannot persuade him to give you the deed, then get the original promise in writing. His verbal promise is not good. He never has to sell. After you get it in writing, try to put a reasonable time limit on the sale, but not so early as to cause a forced sale.

He might trick you by renting the home. Try to stay in the home as long as you need it for the childrens' feeling of security. It's bad enough they are losing a father image. There is no reason for adding to the loss, unless you and the children have good and compelling reasons for wanting to move out of the house.

Have him agree to offer the home for sale several months before you plan to move out. You are protecting whatever interest you have in the home by remaining in it.

I advise every wife to make certain that the title to the home is placed in both names as tenants by the entirety with right of survivorship. Remember, when marriage dies, romance flies. Protect yourself while the romance is alive.

Q: Suppose the couple cannot agree about some items in their property settlement. Who makes the decisions?

A: It is not quite the same as custody and child support, where the court will make all the decisions. The court will usually not make decisions on personal or real property in a divorce action. The parties have to go to court with a separate suit, and the court will order a partition suit, which means a forced sale of the properties not agreed on.

This is one of the tragic aspects of divorce. The only people who gain from a forced sale are the lawyers, commissioners, appraisers, and newspapers. The two parties have to engage lawyers, who will argue about the home before a forced sale is possible. The parties have to go back to the commissioner who heard the divorce case, and pay him an additional fee. The commissioner reports to the judge, and another commissioner is appointed to handle the forced sale of the house. He gets at least five percent of the proceeds. The sale has to be advertised, and newspapers have to be paid for the required legal advertising.

In most partition suits one party is willing to buy, but the other is not willing to sell. Three-quarters of the time, or more, one spouse will eventually end up owning the house. Often, unfortunately, one spouse is so bullheaded that he or she does not want the house to be sold at fair market value, which would avoid all those fees.

Q: What if in a partition suit one party is willing to buy the property at fair market value and the other party is willing to sell?

A: There must be an appraisal. The judge has to confirm the sale. He usually wants to see the house sold for the appraised price. But if the highest bid comes in for less, he may confirm the sale. Then both parties receive less, and pay more fees. Or the judge can order the home readvertised, which requires more fees.

Let's say the appraisal is $40,000. If the bid comes in at $30,000, the judge may confirm the bid. If the bid comes in at $15,000, the judge may order a rebid.

Lawyers do not like to get involved in this kind of action with the family home. Here again, the best way is for the spouses to communicate.

Q: Suppose the husband wants to buy the house. Where can he get the money to pay the wife for her one-half share?

A: That is his problem. He has a right to take a second mortgage on the house and pay her with the proceeds. Or, more often she takes a second mortgage, letting him make the monthly payments to her just as he would have made to the mortgage company. He pays her less interest than he would pay the mortgage company but more interest than she could have gotten for the principal sum had she put it into a savings and loan account.

Q: The husband insists on paying bills (utilities, mortgage, medical expenses) and giving his ex-wife money for food and clothing. He owns the home she occupies. Does this situation benefit the wife or husband more?

A: It benefits him more, because he is building up his equity in the home. As the mortgage payments are made, the loan balance is reduced and the home becomes more valuable to him.

He is in the position of a landlord, and she is the position of a tenant. He can evict her at the judge's discretion. If they have no children living in the home, she would have a hard time fighting eviction.

The wife would be wise to insist that her right to remain in the home be spelled out in the separation agreement, and probably made part of the divorce decree.

Q: What if one person moves out of the home or apartment before a separation agreement? What can that party take?

A: The nice thing would be to try to communicate and agree on what each will take. She can take everything that is obviously hers. He can take everything that is obviously his.

If they have a joint checking or savings account, I would advise each spouse not to withdraw more than half.

If the wife leaves and takes items on which the husband still owes money, the husband may not like it, but he is still obligated to pay for them.

If the spouses live in an apartment and both names are on the lease, the landlord cannot change the lock at the request of either party. Neither has the right to lock the other one out; if one party does this, it is called constructive desertion in some states. It is a ground for divorce and can be used against the offender.

Q: Suppose husband and wife are joint owners of a house and both are to share in the profit when it is sold. If the wife and children remain there until the house is sold, who pays for major repairs (leaks, roof, appliances) during that time?

A: If the house is sold as the result of a partition suit (forced sale) ordered by the court, the spouse who pays expenses after separation would first be reimbursed for these expenditures. The remaining net proceeds would be divided equally.

11

Hidden Assets and Income

Q: If I do not know my husband's assets, is there any way of finding out what they are?

A: If you are married and there is no action for anything including divorce between you, the best way to find out is to ask him. If he refuses to tell you, there is not much you can do short of legal action.

If he gives you information that you feel is incomplete or inaccurate, you will not be the first wife with that complaint. He may or may not have valid reasons for withholding the information from you.

In a divorce action, after you have subpoenaed financial statements showing his assets, it is costly and almost impossible to prove the existence of assets he did not list. He will swear under oath that he has listed them all.

But suppose you remember he has papers in an out-of-town safe-deposit box in both your names. You go to the bank, open the box, and examine the contents. If unlisted assets are discovered, he can testify that he forgot the box was there and has not visited it for years. The bank's records will confirm or disprove that statement, because they list the date and time of every visit to the box with the signature of the party opening it.

It is quite likely there will be nothing in the box that will affect your settlement. Even if an unlisted asset is discovered in the box, the most you can get is a portion of it, in addition to the satisfaction of showing the judge that your husband is not entirely honest.

But that does not force your husband to "come clean" about any other assets he failed to list. You will have to prove their existence beyond doubt. This is very costly in time and money.

CASE IN POINT: I know a woman who spent three years, during and after divorce proceedings, hiring detectives, accountants, and lawyers in several states to track down assets that the husband did not list. Instead of working for a living during those three years she kept a vendetta going and spent practically every waking hour on her project. She accumulated a voluminous file and was in and out of court in at least two states with half a dozen lawyers. She even involved her children in her efforts. Had she worked for those three years, she would have earned a minimum of $5,000 to $10,000 each year. Instead, she spent tens of thousands on lawyers, traveling, and private eyes, and suffered personal traumas and alienated her children.

The results of her search were meager and not worth the campaign.

Q: What can lawyers do to help discover hidden assets?

A: Very little. A lawyer can't do much more than what you can do—hire a private detective.

Q: Can a certified public accountant refuse to give either party a copy of a joint tax return or other financial records?

A: Until the law was changed recently, the CPA was not obliged to give a copy of a joint tax return to either spouse. The new law requires him to give a copy of the return to his client, that is, to the spouse who signed the return, but not to the other spouse.

Of course, if both parties are partners in a business and the CPA does the return for both, and the payment for his services is from a partnership checkbook, he would lose his clients if he refused to give them both copies as requested. But once the battle, the divorce proceeding, begins, the CPA even in this situation, can refuse to give the other spouse a copy if he is working for one spouse only.

The returns, as well as other financial data, can be subpoenaed by the court. But the existence and location of the records must be known and pointed out by the party who requests their appearance.

Q: How can a spouse hide assets and income?

A: It is not the purpose of this book to advise dishonest people "how to." But for protection and enlightenment, I will discuss several methods of hiding assets and income—methods well known to most accountants, lawyers, and judges.

1. A spouse can hide cash anywhere: under the mattress, in a drawer, buried in a can in the backyard, buried underground in a vacant lot or other area too large to search.

2. A spouse can open bank accounts in any city in any state or in a foreign country, like Switzerland, where the laws do not permit disclosure except under unusual circumstances. If he or she requests that no statement be mailed out, it will be difficult to track down such bank accounts.

3. Safe-deposit boxes can still be opened in other people's names but banks are beginning to use Social Security numbers, which makes it easier to trace a box. But money can be deposited in the name of a person not known by the spouse.

4. Anticipating a divorce, a corporation executive may deliberately arrange for his salary to be smaller than he deserves. When the court looks at his salary checks, his ability to pay alimony and child support will seem limited. If the culprit then has his salary increased appreciably after the divorce, the other spouse can go back to court and ask for more; often, the court obliges.

5. The assets of a spouse can be minimized; for example, land purchased for $10,000 ten years ago which has been rezoned and is now worth $30,000 will show up in the statement as only a $10,000 asset if the owner uses a cost basis for listing his assets. This

is legal. The aggrieved party can have the properties appraised and convert the figures to fair market value, which gives the court a more realistic picture of net worth.

12

Out-of-State Garnishment

If husband and wife live in a different states, we must distinguish between two types of jurisdiction: jurisdiction on the subject matter *(in rem)* and personal jurisdiction *(in personam)*.

Suppose the wife is in Virginia. When she files for divorce, the husband has moved to North Carolina. She can file for divorce in Virginia if she lived there for the required six months, etc. She can obtain the divorce decree.

But the Virginia court will not decide how much he has to pay her, since it has jurisdiction over only the subject matter, the divorce. She cannot get money unless the court that has personal jurisdiction over her husband, the North Carolina court, awards it.

She must serve him the papers in order to obtain the divorce, but she can get "substituted" service. Instead of the sheriff handing him papers notice can be published in the local newspaper and a copy mailed to his last known address. Note that this type of service is good enough for jurisdiction over the subject matter, but not for personal service.

Now she has her divorce, but no provision has been made for alimony or child support.

If he works for the U.S. government and if she gets an order in Virginia under the Reciprocal Support Act, she can garnishee his wages if he is living in another state. But she can't just write a letter; she has to get a garnishment from the juvenile court.

CASE IN POINT: A navy wife living in Tidewater, Virginia, called me about a garnishment. Navy pay for Tidewater comes from a finance center in Ohio. There is no *local* navy finance center. In order to garnishee the wages, she has to go to the check-issuing source. If she does not go in person, she has to have a garnishment filed in an Ohio court, which will serve papers on the Navy finance center. (The air force finance center is in Denver, Colorado.)

There is another problem. In order to garnishee the navy man's pay for a child-support order, she has to take a valid judgment from Virginia to Ohio and sue on it.

Even though there is a new law that makes it look easy, you can't just fire off a letter and expect some federal clerk to punch a computer saying that the wage is garnisheed and you can expect a check in the next mail. It will cost the wife some time and money to hire lawyers. She will have to find another lawyer in another state, and he is going to charge a fee.

If the new law provided for service of papers locally, she would not have to hire a lawyer for garnishment. If she had a judgment order, she could see a local magistrate and pay $10 or $15; he would forward the local papers to Ohio; and the navy finance center would automatically pay without the intervention of an Ohio judge.

Although the government has been lax in publishing guidelines on exactly how garnishment works, some federal agencies have clarified the procedures. A quote follows from the *Air Force News for Retired Personnel* (March-April 1977).

> *Garnishment of Pay.* Due to numerous inquiries concerning garnishment of pay, we remind that since January 1975 retired pay is subject to court-ordered garnishment or attachment when retirees have been court-ordered to provide child

support or alimony. When the Air Force Accounting and Finance Center receives a writ of garnishment in the form of a civil court order, they must, by law, use retired pay, including any allotments from such pay, to satisfy that amount. The amount can include all retroactive amounts for which a retiree may be delinquent in his child-support or alimony payments. AFAFC will notify the retiree of garnishment proceedings against his pay, and any challenge to this action is strictly a matter between the retiree and the court issuing the garnishment order. If you need to call AFAFC on the subject of garnishment of pay, the number is AC 303-320-7208.

13

Separation Agreements

When Robert F. Kennedy was running for the Democratic nomination for President on an anti-Vietnam War platform, he kept urging, "Let's stop the fighting and talk. We can always start the war again."

This is the best advice you will ever receive if you are unhappy with your marriage, even if you have firmly decided on divorce.

It is a lot to ask and it is hard to do, but, for God's sake, *communicate*. Once you get your quarrel into the hands of lawyers, it is going to be escalated and prolonged. The trauma you go through with lawyers is going to be as bad as the trauma you go through with your husband or wife. If you live in the same home or apartment, even though you may be wearing earplugs, you can at least scream at each other. Once you get into lawyers' hands, you are lucky if they return your phone calls.

So try to get as much as you can settled between you, no matter how upsetting it is, before you make that first visit to the lawyer.

A separation agreement is usually prepared and signed before a divorce. In most states, once a separation agreement has been executed properly, the couple can get a no-fault divorce after a specified period of time. In New York State, for example, the time is one year. In some states the separation agreement can be and should be made part of the court's final decree, lending it the dignity of the court. In New York State 90 percent of all divorces are based on separation agreements without court battles.

The Checklist and Outline below attempts to cover every item that could be included in a separation agreement. Many lawyers I know have called my checklist "a service to lawyers." The list makes it unnecessary to spend time painfully extracting the desires and requirements from the parties in a divorce.

The spouses can read the list together. At least you can tell which items apply to your separation and divorce. Then you can try to *agree* on as many items as possible.

Take the items agreed upon to your attorneys. You may be able to tell them you agree on all except one or two. This is much better than visiting your lawyer and expecting him to get all the facts and make all the decisions for you. Remember, you always know your own affairs better than your lawyer does. People are scared to death of lawyers, and justifiably so. But if you try it this way, you will walk into your lawyer's office a little more confident that you are going to be able to communicate with him, and he will have more respect for you because you have done your homework.

Keep in mind that what you read here is not *your* agreement; it is only an aid. But if no item is overlooked, you may be saved quite a bit of heartache in the future. Make marginal notes on the outline of what you want in each category. Give it to your attorney.

Checklist and Outline

Recitals. This is a preamble, listing date and place of marriage; names and birth dates of children; location and ownership of marital dwelling; whether the parties are now living apart; and the basic purpose of the agreement (to settle between them all their respective rights and duties).

1. *Separation:* The parties agree to live apart and not to molest or interfere with each other in any way.*

2. *Personal property, bank accounts, securities, and household effects:* (An agreed division of these items is set forth.*)

3. *Real property:* (An agreed division is set forth, which may include transfer of title to the marital dwelling to the spouse who has custody of the children; it may add that such party shall have exclusive use of marital dwelling until the children are emancipated (released from parental control) or the spouse remarries or some other specified event occurs. It may set forth a procedure for selling jointly owned real property or for dividing the proceeds in agreed proportions or amounts; how mortgage or other carrying charge payments, made after the date of the agreement but before the sale, are to be credited in such division; and who will pay taxes resulting from the sale.*)

4. *Emancipation event for children:* (This sets forth the age or other event in the children's lives (for example, permanent residence away from custodial parent or entry into the armed forces) that will terminate the obligation to provide child support. Often the age is 18, but may be extended for the completion of four continuous years of college education.*)

5. *Remarriage:* If the party receiving alimony (spousal support) decides to remarry, both parties agree that payments identical to the regular alimony payments will continue for a period of so-and-so-many months. (This partly removes a financial bar to remarriage. Under this arrangement payments after remarriage will no longer be considered alimony from a tax standpoint and will no longer be a tax deduction to the paying party and income to the receiving party. They will be contractual obligations.*)

6. *Allowance for support and maintenance of*

---

*See further notes at the end of the sample agreement.

spouse: (This sets forth the obligation to pay alimony, which may be fixed amounts or on a scale that varies according to cost of living, paying party's income, or decreasing needs of the receiving party as she develops her own earning power (for example, after a period of education, training, or relocation). Alimony payments are deductible to the paying party and taxable to the receiving party. The wife should be advised how taxes on her alimony will reduce her net income.)

7. *Allowance for support and maintenance of children:* (This sets forth the obligation of a parent to pay child support. Usually it provides for fixed periodic payments and an agreement on who will bear extraordinary or nonrecurring expenses (camp, music lessons, psychotherapy). Child-support payments are not deductible by the paying party and not taxable income to the receiving party. See chapter 8.)

Note that the allowance for support and maintenance of the spouse can be combined with that of the children. If the total amount is not broken down, the paying party can deduct the total payment and the receiving party must include it as taxable income. Both parties should consult their accountants to attain the best tax results. (Wealthy individuals may want to establish alimony trusts to satisfy their obligation to support wives and children.)

8. *Custody:* (The custody arrangement may be total control by one parent, joint control over major decisions but with the children living with one parent, or divided custody with the children spending roughly equal time with each parent. Included are visitation rights for the parent who does not have custody during the school year; holidays and vacations; procedures for transferring the children from one parent to the other; the right of each parent to be informed about the whereabouts and conditions of the children when they are with the other parent; specific decisions (surgery, boarding schools) that will require the consent of both parents. A restriction on the right of the parent having custody to move the child's residence more than a lim-

ited distance is frequently included. Enforcement may be questionable, but it can do no harm to include this restriction. See chapter 8.)

9. *Voluntary payments:* (This states that any payments made above the amounts required by the agreement shall not create precedents for the future.*)

10. *College expenses:* (This sets forth how the parties will pay for some or all of the college and postgraduate expenses of the children. Many separation agreements do not include this. Some require a parent to contribute if financial circumstances reasonably permit. Very few create an absolute obligation.*)

11. *Medical insurance:* (This sets forth who will pay for each member of the family, what the coverage will be, and when the obligation terminates.)

12. *Life insurance:* (This obligates the party who provides the primary financial support to obtain and maintain life insurance in an agreed amount, payable to the other spouse and the children. See chapter 16.)

13. *Debts:* (This states who will pay existing debts and that neither spouse will be responsible for new debts incurred by the other.) The wife/husband agrees not to pledge nor use the joint credit of the parties or the separate credit of the other party after 9:00 a.m. on this such-and-such day of such-and-such month and year. If either party breaches this agreement, the aggrieved party has the option of deducting such indebtedness from the alimony due. (A notice in newspapers stating that you will not be responsible for any indebtedness incurred by your spouse is ineffective. You can best protect yourself by writing a certified or registered letter to all creditors you have been paying.*)

14. *Income taxes:* This states who will pay any deficiencies assessed on past joint income tax returns and how refunds will be divided. It may include an agreement to file joint returns until divorced. It may state which parent will *not* claim children as dependents on his tax returns. This is important because

under current law only the parent who claims the children as dependents and with whom the children are living is entitled to a child-care deduction; also, children's medical expenses paid by a parent are deductible only if that parent claims the children as dependents.*)

15. *Counsel fees:* (This sets forth a spouse's obligations to pay the other spouse's lawyer and that the other spouse has no further claim for such fees.)

16. *Reconciliation:* (This provides that a temporary reconciliation of the parties does not void the agreement unless parties agree in writing to cancel the agreement.)

17. *Matrimonial decree:* (This states that some or all the provisions of the separation agreement will be incorporated into the decree of divorce, but changes can be made on account of new circumstances. If alimony is covered in a separate written agreement, the amount of the alimony payments cannot be altered, even by court decree.*)

18. *Releases:* (These are mutual releases of claims on the property and estate of the other party.)

19. *Default in payment and controversies:* (This may provide that if either party sues to enforce a payment provision of the agreement and wins, or achieves the same result by settlement or voluntary compliance after the suit is begun, the sued party shall pay reasonable counsel fees. It may include agreement to arbitrate certain kinds of disputes or issues not covered in the separation agreement.)

20. *Notices:* (This sets forth the addresses to which notices required under the agreement are to be sent.)

21. *General provisions:* (These may include agreement to bind parties and their heirs, executors, and assigns; stipulation that any changes in the agreement must be in writing and signed by the parties to be valid; statement that the agreement is the complete agreement of the parties; agreement on which state law governs the interpretation and enforcement of the agreement; and acknowledgments by both parties that

they have had independent lawyers and accountants, by the parties except those set out in the agreement have acted freely and voluntarily, and have read and understand the agreement; statement that no representations (for example, about income) have been made and that both parties have made full disclosure of their assets; stipulation that the agreement shall be made part of any decree of court and shall be enforceable by the contempt powers of the court.*)

Additional comments on certain clauses of the Checklist and Outline follow.

On point 1 (Separation): If you not only sign this but adhere to it, your lives will be less miserable. If you seek a divorce, sign and date this agreement after you file for divorce.

On point 2 (Personal property, bank accounts, securities, and household effects): The first decision to be made is how to divide the *cash,* if any, that you have on hand and in joint and separate accounts.

Either you agree on how to divide *stocks and bonds* (securities) or you list them as unagreed-upon items.

Household effects are harder to divide even if you try to split everything down the middle. After all, with $100 in cash, it is not too difficult to take $50 each, and ten shares of stock or bonds can be equally divided. But furniture and other items for one household will not usually accommodate two households. If there is one car, the problem is greater than if there are two. Often there are violent arguments over trivial items.

Try to agree on the division. If you take this problem to a lawyer, you will both probably end up with very little.

On point 3 (Real property): The item of real property most often involved in a divorce proceeding is the home. This is very complicated. To many couples it is the most important item after alimony, custody, and child support. Many ramifications of this question are discussed in chapter 10. If you are lucky enough to own income-producing property, it may not be advisable to sell your at home this time. For splitting equities see chapters 19 and 18.

On point 4 (Emancipation event for children): If there are children, there is the important question of when you will no longer be obligated to support them. The law calls a person a child until 18 years of age, but your children may want to go to college or receive some type of specialized training beyond high school, or they may need some form of remedial education after age 18. These are things on which you and your spouse should be able to agree. Then you make your wishes known to the lawyers so they will be spelled out clearly and legally in the separation agreement, rather than let the lawyers determine what to do. Be sure to get the agreement in writing.

On point 5 (Remarriage): Many people assume that alimony stops automatically upon remarriage. It is not always so. And it may be wise to make an agreement under which alimony continues for a specified time after remarriage.

Let's assume a wife is to receive $500 a month until she remarries. At the time of the divorce, she has a life expectancy of 30 years according to the IRS. Five hundred dollars a month for 360 months adds up to $180,000—a lot of alimony. Suppose she dates a man who is not a big money earner. He would like to marry her, but they both know she would lose her alimony. So they live together unmarried, and the ex-husband goes on paying indefinitely.

But the situation is different if she can tell her friend she has an agreement under which her alimony continues for, let's say, five years after she remarries. With this inducement, the two may decide to get married, counting on an improvement in their earnings before the alimony payments run out.

I am not suggesting how long the payments should last or how high they should be. In the case under discussion, I would be delighted to say, "If you remarry within five years, I will continue to pay you the same $500 a month for another five years." Instead of paying for 30 years, I pay her for ten.

There is nothing wrong with offering an inducement for one's ex-wife to remarry. And it certainly is not against public policy.

On point 9 (Voluntary payments): The husband may at times feel warm and generous toward his former spouse or his children, and may make occasional or periodic gifts to them over and above his contractual and legal obligations. These actions *might* not be used against him if this provision is incorporated into the separation agreement. I say might not. I recently had a bitter experience with the Supreme Court of Virginia which completely ignored contractual obligations in favor of behavioral patterns. My generous act were contradictory to the terms of the contract, and so I was penalized. As a result I reluctantly advise that you curb your generosity and adhere strictly to the terms of your agreement. But if you must be generous, make this provision as strong and as clear as possible.

On point 10 (College expenses): The separation agreement should also designate who makes the final decisions about the education of the children.

On point 13 (Debts): There is much misunderstanding about how debts should be handled. As I said, taking an ad in the paper will not protect you; often the court will provide protection. Let's assume there is a separation agreement; the wife goes out and, by the time the agreement is recorded or becomes effectual, she uses their joint credit cards and buys thousands of dollars worth of merchandise. The judge may deduct the amount she spent from her alimony award. Furthermore, her action may prejudice the judge against her during the entire proceedings.

On point 14 (Income taxes): Be certain to spell the agreement out in detail. Pay all the income taxes due by the date of the separation agreement. The paying party should be entitled to any refund as of the same date. (See also chapter 7.)

On point 17 (Matrimonial decree): You really need a lawyer on this one.

On point 21 (General provisions): All these provisions are important. Omission of any of them can prove costly.

COMMUNICATE BEFORE YOU LITIGATE!

14

Separation or Divorce?

If two people want freedom from each other, there may be advantages in obtaining a legal separation sanctioned by court decree. It is often called "divorce from bed and board"—desirable in particular if there are no children. Or a married couple can just stop living together with or without a written or verbal separation agreement.

They may reason that they need more space or more privacy—that one or both feel smothered. They may not be certain they want to obtain a divorce. They may obtain a legal separation feeling someone more eligible is out there, but they do not want to date openly while they are legally together, and do not want to be guilty of adultery. After legal separation each can explore the outer world with no fear of public disfavor.

If either finds a more likely partner and desires a new marriage, then divorce is in order. After separation and the passage of time required by the state in which they live, divorce can be legally routine.

If after some time they discover that they *had* better than what they *found,* they can reunite without having suffered the expense and hardship of a divorce.

They can still date each other. Many well-known couples marry, divorce, date, and get along much better than during their marriage.

Legal separation is an easy way to avoid getting

married to someone else. It is used as an excuse all the time: "Honey, I'd like to marry you, but I can't. I'm already married. But that won't stop us from seeing each other, because I am legally separated."

There can be considerable financial advantages. The couple may live in a community property state. He has a business with a large net worth; she has very little to offset his business assets in case of a community property split. The business is not divisible, and he does not have cash enough to pay her off and still keep it solvent.

They make a financial arrangement. She receives separate maintenance. He runs his business. Each lives his or her own life without reproach, and if he dies, she automatically gets whatever share of the estate their agreement or the law prescribes.

And legal separation may be easier than divorce on the children, who can always hope for reconciliation, which is more probable after separation than after divorce.

Thousands of legally separated men are living with other women who often have children of their own. Visitation rights seem to work out about the same either way.

The Roman Catholic Church and some others completely disapprove of divorce. Separation, legal or otherwise, may be the only acceptable answer.

If you cannot reach a separation agreement, you are both in trouble. The judge, in most states, will make the decisions on alimony (spousal support) and child support and custody. But in some states, where the judge cannot decide for you about property, you may be faced with the horror of horrors, the *forced sale*. (See chapters 10 and 13.)

There can be a legal separation with the spouses living under the same roof but not sharing the same bed. For example, the children love the neighborhood and school, and the husband will not leave, because he loves his children.

Something like this often happens, especially when

the couple are getting ready for a no-fault divorce. They move into separate bedrooms.

But be careful. The question is whether they continue the sexual relationship. There is an old legal expression, "You can't copulate by night and litigate by day." It is going to be difficult to convince a judge that a married couple lives in the same house and have not been making love. Separation is more easily provable if the couple are physically separated.

CASE IN POINT: When I was going through my second divorce, my lawyer warned me not to let my wife get me in bed with her. He stated that if we had sexual relations, it would wipe out any grounds for divorce I had against her for acts committed before that date.

Her lawyer must have advised her of the necessity of getting me in bed with her and of proving the fact. She tried several ruses to accomplish this.

The judge would not order her out of my house. So I put a lock on every door. I had my son sleep in the house in order to witness the fact that I locked myself in my bedroom every night.

There is no unanimity on this point, but it is obvious that my case against her would have been considerably weakened if the judge believed that I was belligerent toward her in court but affectionate and tender with her in bed.

If a husband refuses to leave the home and the wife is therefore the one who leaves, it is going to hurt her divorce. She will have to prove that he put her in fear of grave bodily harm. Fear of mental or physical cruelty could be grounds for *desertion*.

Don't have the separation agreement state that both parties can live with other people without consequences. You are supposed to come into court with "clean hands," and if you go into court with such an agreement, traditionally the woman will look worse than the man. It is not a matter of equity or justice, but of how the judge will view the agreement. I advise the woman to be discreet and to refrain from putting anything in writing indicating that she wants the right to live with another person before she is divorced.

PART THREE

Special Agreements

15

Premarital Agreements

A premarital (or antenuptial) agreement is an instrument that spells out in detail what each person can expect from marriage in terms of finances and property during the marriage and in the event of the other spouse's death.

In particular entering second or third marriages, people have vested rights they want to protect. A premarital agreement is essential where there are children by former marriages and/or an estate.

In the last few years, premarital agreements have become increasingly popular and broad in scope.

But they have also become increasingly ridiculous, forcing the courts to throw out a large number of them. For example, with the emergence of feminism, women try to marry with contracts that spell out which spouse will do the diapers or dishes, keep the books, babysit, and mow the lawn. Some agreements go so far as to specify that he will not mention her weight nor she the wart on his nose.

Lawyers charge from a few hundred to a few thousand dollars for drawing up premarital agreements. Ethical lawyers will explain to their clients that the scope of the agreement should be limited to dividing property and other assets. "Frivolous" clauses may negate the entire agreement.

In many states more of these agreements have

been attacked and set aside than have been sustained. A premarital agreement is a technical legal instrument best devised by attorneys. No person without legal background should attempt it.

The basis of a premarital agreement is full disclosure by both parties of all their assets. If the husband-to-be is wealthy, his attorney would be well advised to tell the prospective wife to engage an accountant and an attorney of her own.

Both parties should surrender complete, up-to-date financial statements. Both parties and their attorneys and accountants should state in writing that they have examined the financial statements and understand them.

They can establish a trust fund to continue payments to the survivor after the death of a spouse. Many written agreements stipulate that alimony will not survive the death of the paying party. A provision for this type of trust fund protects the recipient against this possibility (See chapter 21.)

As an example of what to do and what not to do, I offer two premarital agreements. Agreement No. 1 was made between my second wife and me. No. 2 is a revised agreement, in which we'll use Mary Smith as the wife's name; I worked on it with five attorneys from different states, using the same basic facts. It is adapted to New York State law. Read the discussion that follows Agreement No. 2, then see how many things you can find wrong with Agreement No. 1.

Premarital Agreement No. 1

AGREEMENT made this 6th day of October, 1973, between David I. Levine, of Norfolk, Virginia, and Doris Gibson Condrey, of Norfolk, Virginia.

WHEREAS David I. Levine and Doris Gibson Condrey intend to be married within a short time, and

WHEREAS David I. Levine has disclosed to Doris Gibson Condrey the nature and extent of his various property interests and of his sources of income, and

WHEREAS David I. Levine desires to make a reasonable and sufficient provision for Doris Gibson Condrey in release of and in full satisfaction of all rights which after the solemnization of their marriage Doris Gibson Condrey might or could have, by reason of the marriage, in the property which David I. Levine now has or may hereafter acquire, or in his estate upon his death, and

WHEREAS Doris Gibson Condrey desires to accept this provision in lieu of all rights which she would otherwise acquire, by reason of the marriage, in the property or estate of David I. Levine,

It is therefore agreed:

1. *Release of dower.* David I. Levine shall hold all real property which he now owns or may hereafter acquire free from any claim of dower, inchoate or otherwise, on the part of Doris Gibson Condrey, and this agreement shall evidence the right of David I. Levine to convey any of his real estate free from any such claim of dower. At the request of David I. Levine, Doris Gibson Condrey shall execute, acknowledge, and deliver such other instruments as may be reasonable, required to accomplish the transfer by David I. Levine of any of his real property free from any claim of dower in such property.

2. *Payment from estate.* If Doris Gibson Condrey survives David I. Levine as his lawful widow, there shall be paid to her from the estate of David I. Levine, free from all estate, inheritance, succession, or other death taxes, an amount equal to one-third of the value of the net personal property after payment of all debts, taxes, and administrative costs of the estate of David I. Levine, and an amount equal to a one-third life estate in the value of all real estate owned by David I. Levine at the time of his death. Until so paid, such shall constitute a charge upon the entire estate of David I. Levine.

3. *Release of marital rights.* Doris Gibson

Condrey shall accept the provisions in paragraph 2 in release and in full satisfaction of all rights which, by reason of the marriage, she may acquire in the property or estate of David I. Levine, and in consideration thereof she does hereby waive and relinquish all rights which, as widow of David I. Levine, she would otherwise acquire in his property or estate, under the law now or hereafter in effect in any jurisdiction, whether by way of dower, distributive share, right of election to take against a will, widow's allowance, or otherwise.

4. *Disclosure of facts.* Doris Gibson Condrey acknowledges that the present approximate net worth of David I. Levine has been fully disclosed to her, that she understands that such net worth is in excess of $1 million, that she has given consideration to these facts, and that she is entering unto this agreement freely and with a full understanding of its provisions.

5. *Effective date.* This agreement shall come into effect only if the contemplated marriage between David I. Levine and Doris Gibson Condrey is solemnized, and upon coming into effect shall bind, and inure to the benefit of, the parties and their respective heirs, executors, and administrators.

In witness whereof the parties have signed, sealed, and acknowledged this instrument.

[Signatures and seals.]

Premarital Agreement No. 2

THIS AGREEMENT made between David I. Levine [residence], herein called Levine, and Mary Smith [residence], herein called Smith. [If wife is the wealthy one, consider her as "Levine" and him as "Smith."]

WITNESSETH: The parties are about to marry. In anticipation thereof, they desire to fix and determine by premarital agreement the rights and claims that will accrue to each of them in the estate and property of the other by reason of the marriage, and to accept the provisions of this agreement in lieu of and in full discharge, settlement, and satisfaction of all rights and claims.

NOW, THEREFORE, in consideration of the premises and of the marriage, and in further consideration of the mutual promises and undertakings hereinafter set forth, the parties agree:

1. Smith shall receive and accept from Levine's estate after his death, subject to the conditions set forth in clause 3 hereof, in place and stead of, and in full final settlement and satisfaction of, any and all rights and claims which she might otherwise have had in Levine's estate and property under any statute or statutes now or hereafter in force in this or any other jurisdiction, whether by way of her right of election to take against Levine's will, her share of the estate in intestacy, or otherwise, the following:

(A) A sum equal to one-third of the following amount: the value at the time of his death of all of the personal property in the estate of Levine less all estate and inheritance taxes attributable to such property; and

(B) A life estate in one-third of an amount equal to the value of the real property in the estate of Levine at the time of his death less all estate and inheritance taxes due on such property, to be computed as follows: (1) the real property in Levine's estate shall be valued by an appraiser selected by the executor and the wife. If the executor and the wife cannot agree on the appraiser, then a mutually agreeable third party shall name the appraiser. The appraisal should be made within 90 days after death of Levine; (2) estate and inheritance taxes attributable on a pro rata basis to such property shall be computed and deducted from said valuation and the result divided by three; (3) The amount payable to Smith hereunder shall be the interest at the rate of [average net annual return of the real property] percent per annum of the aforesaid sum, discounted to present value at the rate of six percent per year, for a successive number of years beginning in the year of Levine's death and equal to [average or mean life expectancy of Smith, e.g., 73 years] less Smith's age at the time of Levine's death.

2. Subject to the conditions specified in paragraph 3 below, the amounts due pursuant to paragraph 1 hereof, shall be paid as follows:

(A) [Amount] thereof within 30 day after the probate of Levine's will but in no event later than 60 days after his death;

(B) [Amount] thereof within six months after Levine's death, and

(C) the balance within 12 months after Levine's death.

3. It is of the essence of this agreement that Smith shall be entitled to receive, and shall receive, the aforesaid sums if and only if (a) she survives Levine and (b) the parties are married and living together at the time of Levine's death. Or, if either party is suing for divorce, and a separation agreement has not been signed by both parties, then this agreement prevails. If Smith does not survive Levine, or if the parties were not married at the time of Levine's death, Smith shall not be entitled to receive any sum whatsoever from Levine's estate; and in such event, her waiver and release of any and all rights and claims she may have had in Levine's estate, as more particularly set forth in clause 4 hereof, shall be of full force and effect and shall be conclusive and binding on her.

4. Smith hereby waives and releases any and all rights and claims of every kind, nature, and description that she may acquire as Levine's surviving spouse in his estate upon his death, including (but not by way of limitation) any and all rights in intestacy, and any and all rights of

election to take against Levine's last will and
testament under section 5–1.1 of the Estates,
Powers, and Thrusts Law of the State of New
York, any law amendatory thereof or supplementary or similar thereto, and the same or similar
law of any other jurisdiction. This provision is
intended to and shall serve as a waiver and release of Smith's right of election in accordance
with the requirements of section 5–1.1 of the
Estates, Powers, and Trusts Law of the State of
New York.

5. Smith acknowledges that she has certain
property of her own. Levine hereby waives and
releases any and all rights and claims of every
kind, nature, and description that he may acquire
as Smith's surviving spouse in her estate upon her
death, including (but not by way of limitation)
any and all rights in intestacy, and any and all
rights of election to take against Smith's last will
and testament under section 5–1.1 of the Estates,
Powers, and Trusts Law of the State of New
York, any law amendatory thereof or supplementary or similar thereto, and the same or similar law of any other jurisdiction. This provision
is intended to and shall serve as a waiver and
release of Levine's right of election in accordance
with the requirements of section 5–1.1 of the
Estates, Powers, and Trusts Law of the State of
New York.

6. Each party shall during his or her life-
time keep and retain sole ownership, control, and
enjoyment of all property, real and personal, now
owned or hereafter acquired by him or her, free
and clear of any claim by the other, including
community property.

7. The consideration for this agreement is
the mutual promises herein contained and the
marriage about to be solemnized. If the marriage
does not take place, this agreement shall be in
all respects and for all purposes null and void.

8. Each party shall, upon the other's request, take any and all steps and execute, acknowledge, and deliver to the other party any
and all further instruments necessary or ex-

pedient to effectuate the purpose and intent of this agreement.

9. Smith hereby acknowledges that Levine has fully acquainted her with his means and resources; that he has informed her in detail that his net worth as of the date hereof is [amount]. As is set forth in a financial statement attached hereto and made a part hereof [exhibit number and date] and is signed by the parties hereto; that she has ascertained and weighed all the facts, conditions and circumstances likely to influence her judgment herein; that all matters embodied herein as well as all questions pertinent hereto have been fully and satisfactorily explained to her; that she has given due consideration to such matters and questions; that she clearly understands and consents to all the provisions hereof; that she has had the benefit of the advice of counsel of her own selection; and that she is entering into this agreement freely, voluntarily, and with full knowledge.

10. This agreement contains the entire understanding of the parties. There are no representations, warranties, promises, covenants, or undertakings, oral or otherwise, other than those expressly set forth herein.

11. This agreement shall inure to the benefit of and shall be binding upon the heirs, executors, and administrators of the parties.

[Date, signatures of parties, attorneys, and accountants, and seals.]

According to Agreement No. 1, if I died with no will and no descendants (children and/or lineal descendants), my wife could inherit my entire estate.

Virginia is one of the few states that has dower rights. Every time I want to sell property or deed an easement, the recipient will want my wife to sign away her dower rights even though I acquired the property long before I met her and the property was recorded in my name only.

Suppose I want to dispose of property, and my wife, for any reason, refuses to sign. Taking her to court is not exactly a manifestation of love and trust. I have known property owners and their lawyers to forge the wife's name when she refused to sign deeds, resulting in disbarment for the lawyers and forgery charges against the husbands. Many property owners in dower states have been ruined.

"Payment from estate" (paragraph 2) does not necessarily protect the widow. The husband could dispose of personal property (monies, stocks, bonds, furniture) at any time before his death. Although a superficial reading can lead one to think that the widow is going to get one-third of the real estate, she is getting only a one-third life estate in the value of all real estate, which could be less, depending on her age at the time of his death.

"Disclosure of facts" (paragraph 4) is poorly done because all the wife would have to do is go into court and swear that she was not given full disclosure and that "in excess of $1 million" could be $2 million or $200 million. She could also claim (in many cases, rightfully so) that the financial statement, though given to her, was beyond her capacity to grasp, being too complex.

When I had my first hearing before the judge in my divorce action against Doris, I was shocked when he asked my attorney if there was any premarital agreement between us and my attorney answered no. I didn't want to call my own attorney a liar in front of the judge. What made him deny the existence of the agreement of October 6, 1973? It is obvious to me now that he never should have drawn the agreement and gotten her to sign it without having insisted that she engage an attorney to represent her in the matter. The law customarily interprets an ambiguous instrument against the party whose attorney drew up the instrument. Since my attorney had drawn up the agreement for both of us, he knew it could do me little or no good.

The revised agreement is a much better instrument. But any written premarital agreement is better than a verbal one.

Note that in a premarital agreement there is no minimum percentage of a man's estate that must be provided for a woman. No matter what a premarital agreement says, it does not prevent the husband from giving away all his properties, both personal and real, to a person not his wife; his wife has very little protection here.

16

Life Insurance

It is amazing how many people don't understand the tax ramifications of life insurance. There are three terms that are important to understand. When there is an insurance policy on my life I am the *insured*. The person who collects the insurance money when I die is the *beneficiary*. All of you know that. But few people understand the significance of the *ownership* of a policy. Usually the person who is insured owns the policy, but I want to make it clear that a policy owned by the husband can be a very bad deal for the wife if he dies or if there is a divorce. The more heavily insured person should not be the owner of the policy.

What does it mean if my wife is the owner of the policy? I still pay the premiums (legally, it doesn't matter who pays them). She is the beneficiary and the owner. Suppose I want to divorce her, and I decide to stop paying the premiums and cancel the policy. I cannot cancel it, because she owns it. She can continue paying the premiums and keep the insurance in force even if we are divorced. There is no way that I could stop her from doing this. I can't threaten her with canceling the policy and collecting the cash surrender value if she is the owner.

Finally, when an insured dies, the owner (who is also the beneficiary) pays no inheritance tax on the life-insurance payments received.

17

Community Property

The community property states—Arizona, California, Idaho, Louisiana, Nevada, New Mexico, Texas, and Washington—divide property that has been accumulated by the parties during marriage between them in case of divorce.

These states recognize three categories of property:

1. *The husband's separate property:* All property, real and personal, that he owned before the marriage, and any income that property has produced since the marriage; and property he is given or inherits during the marriage, plus assets such property generates.

He can do whatever he likes with his property. His wife has no claim on his separate property during marriage, after divorce, or after his death.

2. *The wife's separate property:* What applies to the husband (above) applies equally to the wife.

3. *Community property:* All other property acquired during the marriage is community property. By law the husband and wife are partners in the ownership of the properties and in any increment (increase in value) resulting therefrom.

There are borderline cases. In general, the time factor dominates as indicated above. Another factor, called tracing, is a complex legal concept that traces the origin of property to determine whether it is community property.

The relative contributions of the spouses to the acquisition of community property are not recognized. (These are the states where kitchen and diaper labor are equated with work outside the home.) If the wife earns more than the husband, the husband still owns half of the property as long as they are married.

The great advantage to the wife in a community property state is that the courts will divide the property upon divorce. In many noncommunity property states the courts will only decide alimony and child support; since they will not divide property, disagreements often result in disastrous forced sales of property.

Division of property in community property states is not as rigid as one might think. In Idaho and Texas judges are not compelled to divide the property equally. They exercise the same discretion in property divisions that judges in other states have in determining alimony and child support; they will consider the relative financial condition of the parties, their ages and physical conditions, who is at fault in breaking up the marriage, relative abilities and future needs, and so on.

Nor does the wife necessarily have equal rights in community property states. In Louisiana, for example, the wife has no control over management of community property as long as the couple are married. Barring fraud, the husband can buy, manage, and sell without consulting her. The results of his management or mismanagement will increase or decrease her share of community property. (The same is true in Idaho, except that her earnings remain her separate property.)

In the other community property states the undivided half share of community property can be disposed of by either party by will.

18

How to Split Equities
upon Marriage

This is mainly a question of taxes. If two people marry and neither has any equities (cash, real estate, bonds, and other things of value), there are no tax problems because there is nothing to tax. But suppose she has an interest in an apartment project which has a $50,000 equity—its worth after subtracting the mortgages. She says to her fiancé, "I love you very much, and I know this marriage is going to last. I would like to transfer half of what I have to you, so I am going to give you half of my $50,000 interest, which is $25,000."

First, I'd advise her not to give him anything of value before marriage, because if she is that wealthy and he is that poor, he may be marrying her for money. If he receives a large gift before they marry, there may be no marriage. (However, if one spouse gives the other a ring or other property in anticipation of the marriage and the recipient breaks the marriage off, the law calls it an *inter vivos* gift. If there is fraud, misrepresentation, and/or misunderstanding, the recipient can be sued and forced to return the gift.)

More important is the tax advantage if they wait until after marriage. Under the new tax law which went into effect January 1, 1977, either spouse can make an untaxed gift to the other of up to $100,000. It is to their advantage to wait until they are married and then make the transfer.

There is nothing unethical about legitimately arranging your financial affairs, marital or other, so that the least possible amount of taxes will be paid. One of our great judges, in a tax shelter case, stated that if there are two identical bridges crossing a stream side by side and one of them is toll-free, you would be a fool to take the toll bridge.

Even if you are not wealthy, if you are making payments on a modest home you have a tax shelter. Your real estate taxes and interest payments are tax shelters. Whether poor or wealthy, you'd be foolish not to take deductions to which you are legally entitled.

19

How to Split Equities upon Divorce

Let's consider income-producing property and vacant land.

Residential income properties often consist of rental apartments or homes. Commercial and industrial income properties include retail stores, factories, and warehouses. Usually residential income properties are leased for shorter periods of time than commercial or industrial properties.

If the wife is going to leave town after the divorce, or if she doesn't know much about the properties and an agent is going to handle her rentals, she would be well advised to choose the commercial and/or industrial properties as her share of the equities to be divided. They will afford her more security and less likelihood of vacancies, with less maintenance problems and complaints.

On the other hand, we are in an inflationary market. Taxes, repairs, and other expenses are continually rising. Long-term commercial rental leases with no escalation clauses (provisions for tenants to pay their share of increases in taxes, insurance, and maintenance) have ruined many property owners.

Consult your banker, lawyer, and accountant before making a decision; but, as is true of the law, the more you know about your property, the more intelligently you can discuss it and the less likely you are to accept poor advice—indiscriminately handed out by bankers, lawyers, and accountants every day. Doris Day and many others in the high-income brackets have been defrauded of millions of dollars. They now admit they should have known more about their affairs. So a little homework on your part before you sign any papers is well worth the time and effort.

Vacant land is another matter. If you do not need cash and if you have plenty of income from other sources, your best investment is land. It is not as quickly salable as stocks, diamonds, or even buildings. But land is the commodity from which most others flow. It is the only commodity that cannot increase in total quantity; therefore, as the earth's population increases, land becomes more valuable. Historically, land has been the most important factor influencing the actions of man. Heads of state have risked thousands of lives in order to acquire land but have never surrendered land in order to acquire more people. Land is the best hedge against inflation.

I have worked up an example of assets that you own with your husband; I assume you are entitled to an equal division. (But be sure your state is not among the few that do not recognize equitable division of property.)

Assets of John and Mary Doe to Be Divided 50–50 for Purposes of Divorce

ASSETS

Current Assets (cash and items convertible to cash)

cash in all banks (list banks and account numbers)	$10,000	
100 shares of (name stock) at market $10	1,000	
accounts receivable—in 60 days for goods sold	2,000	
federal tax refund due in 90 days	1,000	
note receivable in 120 days	1,000	$ 15,000

Household effects divided equally (furniture, etc.)

Personal Property		
1956 Oldsmobile, market value	$ 200	
1972 Ford, market value	800	$ 1,000
Fixed Assets (long-term assets)		
Home	$30,000	
4 residential rental units	40,000	
1 commercial rental unit	10,000	
1 industrial rental unit	10,000	
1 20-acre farm (appraised value)	20,000	
Total Fixed Assets		$110,000
Total Assets		$126,000

LIABILITIES (DEBTS)

Current Liabilities (money owed within 12 months)

owed to bank in 120 days	$ 3,000	
furniture, clothes, etc.	3,000	$ 6,000

Long-Term Liabilities (payable over years)

Home	$10,000
4 residential rental units	30,000
1 commercial rental unit	5,000
1 industrial rental unit	5,000

	$ 50,000
Total Liabilities	$ 56,000
NET WORTH (subtract liabilities from assets)	$ 70,000

You are entitled to half of the net worth, or $35,000. You can agree to take any combination of net assets totaling $35,000. If you are from a wealthy family and are not going to face financial strain, you might want the farm plus the $15,000 cash (and items convertible to cash). If you have children, and want to remain in the home, take it. Note that as a net asset it counts as $30,000 (under assets) minus $10,-000 (under liabilities), or $20,000; you are entitled to $15,000 more in net assets.

There are many possible combinations even with simple estates. Only you know what is best for you: competent professionals can advise you best if you go to them with some knowledge and rationality.

My advice to every woman who is divorcing and is not independently wealthy is: Take what you can *now*. Do not place much faith in alimony or child support. Take less if you have to, and cut it clean. You will end up in better shape financially, emotionally, and physically. Do not base your future settlement on his past or present earnings—his financial status may change. Remember, he also is going through a traumatic experience which may leave scars that will affect his future earnings. If he marries another woman with children, he will be less inclined to meet his financial obligations to you. It is only human to resent a former spouse to whom one has to make payments for a long time.

20

Annuities

For those who have children and are fortunate enough to own income-producing properties, the problem of splitting equities is more complex.

Problem: Your wife and you are working on your separation agreement. You own 128 apartments in your names; it is not a corporation. The apartments you own jointly are not salable at a good price because she is going to Las Vegas to get a six-week divorce; it takes time to get the right price for property. She is going to marry another man, who has children, after you are divorced.

You do not want to buy her undivided half interest in the apartments and she does not want to buy yours. (This could be for many reasons. You might not have the cash and might want a complete settlement with no promises of future payments, or there could be complicated tax problems precluding sale— see your accountant on this.)

You have two children, a son and a daughter. You want to be sure your wife does not transfer her half ownership in the apartments to her new husband (you do not want him as a partner), and you want to be sure she does not will the apartments to her new husband or his relatives. And it is obvious that you are not going to be very amicable in the future.

The best way to handle this problem is to set up a joint-and-survivor annuity.

As an example, there follow the exact figures worked out on an apartment project my first wife and I owned in 1972. (The computations would be slightly different today because of IRS modifications.)

Joint-and-Survivor Annuity

The Hodges Manor Apartments, completed July 1, 1969, and composed of 128 units, have an average net cash flow (cash less mortgage payments, interest, and other expenses) of $50,000 per year. The owners (husband and wife) are building apartment projects in excess of 100 units per year; the original mortgage was $940,000.

Cost of raw land	$ 27,500	
Cost of improvements	912,500	
Value of property to be sold (cost basis)		$940,000
Less maximum accelerated depreciation taken (component parts method)		330,946
Adjusted basis		$609,054

It is planned to sell the property to the children on December 31, 1975, after 6½ years of depreciation.

Fair market value	$1,300,000	
Less adjusted basis	609,054	
Gain on sale . . . of which		$690,946
Ordinary income (accelerated depreciation to be recaptured) is	$ 166,721	
Long-term capital gain is	524,225	
Fair market value	$1,300,000	
Less mortgage value at date of sale	820,269	
Present value of annuity		$479,731

The husband's life expectancy in 1975 (age 57) is 20.3 years; the wife's (age 50) is 29.6 years. The expectancy for *either* remaining alive is 32.6 years. In purchasing an annuity, future interest must be discounted: to accumulate the same amount at six percent interest that would accumulate in 32.6 years with *no* interest takes 14.2 years. Then the present value of the annuity ($479,731) divided by 14.2 years gives $33,780 as the yearly annuity payment.

Note that the expected return of the annuity is $33,780 for 32.6 years, or $1,101,228.

Of the yearly annuity payment, 76 percent ($25,-672.80) is taxed as capital gains and 24 percent ($8,107.20) as ordinary income. Note there are no capital gains in the year of sale.

One of the main advantages of another kind of annuity, the private annuity, is that you can use it to remove the property transferred from the husband's and wife's taxable estate.

Advantages to parents

1. There is no inheritance, estate, or gift tax.

2. There is no taxable gain at the time of transfer, because the parents' life span is uncertain, making the total value of the annuity indeterminate. The total value of the annuity can be determined only after the deaths of the parents.

3. Parents retain management if the annuity is carefully worked out.

4. Children can will the property back to the parents.

5. Two or more couples can set the annuity up (but this is cumbersome).

6. If the children die before the parents, the children's estates are liable for the annuity payments.

7. The parents don't have to worry about building up enough equity to take care of estate taxes.

8. Family incomes average out (parents are usually in higher tax brackets, children in lower brackets); total family taxes are less.

9. If one or both of the parents are lucky enough to outlive the theoretical survivors' life expectancy, they receive annuity payments for the rest of their lives *tax-free*.

10. Best of all, if you have capital invested in the property at the time of transfer, the capital comes back to you in the form of your annuities before you have to make any tax payments.

Advantages to children

1. The children now own the property outright, and this part of estate is not subject to diminution of value, because no taxes are involved.

2. They can take the maximum depreciation based on fair market value (what a willing buyer will pay a willing seller).

3. Inflation *helps* them in that the value of the property and the cash flow will increase while the annuity payments remain fixed.

4. If the parents die after three years, and before the theoretical survivors' life expectancy, the children own all the property free and clear.

Cautionary advice

1. The annuity must be at least equal the fair market value. If, for example, the fair market value is $1,300,000 and the parents sell the apartments to the children for $1,000,000, the IRS will assess the parents gift tax on $300,000.

2. Conversely, if the parents sell the apartments to the children for more than the fair market value, the children will have to pay gift tax on the difference.

3. The promise to pay cannot be enforced.

4. The annuity cannot qualify if any party thereto is already dealing with annuities. For example, if a life-insurance company is involved, all the gain will be taxable in the year of the transfer.

5. Transfer cannot be made in contemplation of death (three-year rule).

6. To succeed in this type of venture, you must follow the IRS code word for word.

Annuities are complicated. If you are interested in getting your equities into your children's hands with minimum tax payments, while completely avoiding inheritance tax, take these pages to your lawyers and accountants as valuable guidelines.

21

Wills and Trusts

If you own anything of value, you should have a will. Possessions normally increase during a marriage; yet many couples never think of making a will although enough assets have accumulated to justify one. A very simple will requires no attorney, banker, trustee, or accountant. It requires only a pencil or pen and paper, and it must be in handwriting, not typewritten. It is called a holographic will. It must be dated and be written in contemplation of death. This does not mean that you have to be ill and know when you are going to die, but only that you intend to leave your possessions to others only at death, not before.

Some states that accept holographic wills do not require any witnesses; others do. But I advise you to have your handwritten will witnessed by two or three disinterested, reputable people who have nothing to gain from your will. This is primarily to prevent the handwriting from being challenged. (Howard Hughes left many wills—or many have been claimed to be legitimate—and handwriting experts have been called in to authenticate them.)

Here is a simple example of a holographic will where you have one child and want the child to inherit everything you have:

I, David I. Levine, being of sound and disposing mind and memory, give, devise, and bequeath all

107

of my estate, both real and personal, to my beloved daughter, Jane Smith. [Signature, witnesses'
signatures, and date.]

This will is perfectly legal. If you have two children, you can say "one-half each of my estate to my
beloved daughter, Jane Smith, and to my beloved son,
David I. Levine, Jr." Or you can specify certain items
to go to certain individuals or organizations. You can
leave your furniture to your daughter, your car to your
son, and your home to your church.

If the will is more complicated, seek professional
help. Do not try to do it yourself unless it is as simple
as outlined above.

You can change your will as often as you desire.
Try to update your will whenever there is a substantial
change in your estate.

Your will should be in a safe-deposit box or somewhere safe where it cannot be found by someone who
would benefit from its destruction. Do not leave it
in your dresser drawer. You may die suddenly. (Suppose you leave as much as possible to your children
and try to leave your husband as little as the law al-
lows. He finds the will in the dresser drawer, reads
it, destroys it, and claims his legal one-third of the estate. The children are unaware of the existence of the
will—or even if they have seen it, their word in court
is going to be questioned. So eliminate possible conflict.
You can have copies of the will at home or in your office to be sure that when you die it will be known that
you left a will.)

One mistake is often made by someone who has
written a holographic will leaving everything to the husband or wife. Let's say that eight years ago the wife
drew up a will and left everything to her husband,
placing the original in her safe-deposit box and keeping
a copy in the desk drawer where she worked. Over the
years she accumulated a large estate. She dies. Her
husband marries again. His new wife is greedy and has
children of her own. The children of the first wife in-

herit practically nothing. This obviously was not the first wife's intention.

If you are satisfied to have your spouse inherit one-third of your estate and your children two-thirds, do not draw up a will. Percentages vary. (See chapter 29.) That is called dying intestate (having made no will). The only drawback is that the court must appoint a guardian if the children are minors.

Do not blindly rely on your husband's word that the will he showed you is current. He can keep changing it; and it is the most recent will that will be valid after his death. Often one spouse, in a moment of temporary anger, reduces the other's inheritance. Your best protection is not in a will but in ownership of the assets as they are accumulated during marriage.

There is an old saying, "You can't run things from the grave." But you can make use of trusts. Trusts are set up to have third parties manage estates for the benefit of others. Before divorce, the married couple can leave assets in trust with a bank or other trustee with instructions to ensure that the children will share equally in the distribution of assets. If you have this in mind, see your lawyers, accountants, and bankers. And talk to each other—communicate. The children deserve that much consideration.

One of many kinds of trust is the alimony trust, which should be used only when there is a large estate. The husband places cash and/or properties in the hands of a trustee, to assure the wife that the agreed-upon alimony and child support will be paid continuously.

When deciding to use this vehicle, be sure that your lawyer, accountant, and trustee follow the rules in order to avoid tax problems too complicated to discuss here.

If the following guidelines are adhered to, you will be rather well protected:

1. Every detail of the alimony trust should be spelled out in the separation agreement and signed by both spouses.

2. If possible, have the separation agreement containing the alimony trust provisions incorporated into the final decree of divorce.

3. The separation agreement should cover all your rights and, if there are children, all the provisions for their support.

4. If you and your spouse do not get a final decree of divorce within two years of signing the agreement, the IRS can impose a gift tax on the transfer. If you are still separated, gift tax problems will arise.

Note that these guidelines apply only to the alimony trust section of your separation agreement.

22

Factors in Land Acquisition

Over the past decades, so many thousands of married couples, divorcees, widows, and widowers have been conned into buying valueless land that it has become a national scandal. Victims include illiterates and people with the best education.

If every person who bought land in Florida, Arizona, and other so-called garden spots knew more about what factors make land valuable, there would be much less fraud and resulting heartache.

Following is a list of 32 factors which, in my experience, are important in land acquisition. If you visit the site before you buy land and personally check out the factors on the list, it is almost impossible for you to be cheated.

Any negative factor on the list can render land less valuable; but some compromise may be necessary. If you wait to find land with each factor favorable, you may never be a landowner.

1. Accessibility
2. Air rights
3. Churches
4. Drainage
5. Easements
6. Electricity
7. Financing developments
8. Gas
9. Highway frontage

10. Industry
11. Liens
12. Location
13. Mineral rights
14. Options
15. Political climate
16. Price appraisal
17. Projected land use
18. Restrictions
19. Schools
20. Sewers
21. Shopping
22. Stability of land
23. Surroundings
24. Survey (population)
25. Survey (title)
26. Taxes
27. Terms
28. Topography
29. Transportation
30. Water
31. Waterfront
32. Zoning

And luck.

PART FOUR

Alternatives to Marriage

23

Living Together with No Contract

Census figures show that more than 1 million people are living together without being married. (The average duration of these arrangements is unknown.) I suggest that *several* million people are living together in the United States. Many of us are shocked to learn that this practice is still illegal in most states. Twenty years ago, unmarried people living together was looked upon as a crime. Today, living together is more and more acceptable. Trouble occurs only if someone reports cohabitation and the police feel obligated to investigate.

Many couples who live together marry later. No one can deny that they may understand each other better. But there is no proof that their marriages last longer than marriages of couples who have not lived together.

24

Common-Law Marriage

Alabama, Colorado, Georgia, Idaho, Iowa, Kansas, Michigan, Minnesota, Montana, Ohio, Oklahoma, Pennsylvania, Rhode Island, South Carolina, Texas, and the District of Columbia recognize cohabitation as common-law marriage if two people live together as husband and wife for a certain period of time.

CASE IN POINT: I live in Virginia, a state that does not recognize common-law marriage. Therefore, I can live with a woman without any worry about obligations. Or can I? Virginia does not recognize common-law marriage *unless the sexual relationship began in a state that does recognize common-law marriage.* Then Virginia, that courtly southern state, recognizes the marriage.

It can get more complicated than that. One divorce commissioner in Virginia tried to rule that if a man and a woman living together in Virginia *flew over* a state that recognized common-law marriages, then that constituted common-law marriage in Virginia.

CASE IN POINT: I took a young lady to the District of Columbia and spent a few days there with her. She was legally separated but not divorced. While there, I showed her the outline of this book. I asked her if she noticed anything interesting. She replied, "Yes. We had our first sexual encounter in the District of Columbia, which recognizes common-law marriage. Therefore, if we lived together in Virginia as husband and wife for the prescribed amount of time, we might have a common-law marriage." But on checking this out, I learned that since she was not legally divorced, the criteria for common-law marriage did not apply.

(An interesting sidelight: I asked her why she did not divorce her husband, since, she said, he gave her no alimony and gave her nothing but trouble. She replied, "Well, there is nobody on the scene I want to marry. If I'm lucky and he strikes it rich and dies wealthy, I am going to be entitled to a portion of his estate because I am still legally his wife!")

25

Contract for Living under Separate Roofs

Suppose two people are mutually attracted and desire an intimate relationship, but for some reason do not want to live under the same roof. (She may be legally separated but not divorced; either or both may be parents and feel it would be too risky to expose the other to strange children early in the relationship; she may fear being declared an unfit mother by a former husband who is still bitter because she was awarded child custody.)

She agrees, verbally and tacitly, to perform wifely duties. He may help her financially and otherwise, because he appreciates her efforts to make him happy.

Normally, this type of relationship is even less permanent than marriage or common-law marriage. Either party may become inconsiderate, or more attracted to someone else.

If you want to know if such contracts can have legal standing, see chapter 27.

26

Contract Cohabitation

Several years ago the author of a book called *Contract Cohabitation* reasoned that a man could date at most five women a week or a hundred women a year, trying to find the right one to live with. But if he advertised, he might reach thousands of prospects at once.

His concept is not that far-fetched. (Even Richard Burton announced that during one of his last separations from Elizabeth Taylor he was so lonely that he seriously considered advertising for a prospective mate.)

The author advertised the following working conditions: "$500 per month plus all living expenses. One night a week off and one week a year off."

The number of responses was shocking. He, over 50, received calls from college girls. He received calls and letters from others by the hundreds. And through this medium he did meet a woman with whom he ended up having a pleasant relationship.

I am not advocating this method of finding a mate. On the other hand, I can see nothing wrong with some form of contract cohabitation if you want to share your life with someone but do not want to marry.

There are interesting tax angles to contract cohabitation. Let's consider the financial arrangements. If a woman acts as a man's companion and provides housekeeping and other services for him and he is not charging her rent and is otherwise supporting her, he cannot deduct what he spends on her as an expense.

If she provides services (typing, research, office management) that benefit his business and he pays her $100 per week in addition to taking care of her other expenses, he can deduct only the $100 a week that he is paying for work performed in the office. (I am talking about legitimate work. Don't follow the lead of some well-known congressmen by putting a nontypist on the payroll as your executive secretary.) She has to declare the $100 per week.

If she works in his home rather than his office, doing equivalent work—typing, answering the phone, and so forth—he has to document what she does each minute to justify a tax deduction. He must have a good explanation of what she does if she is both living and working in his home.

Suppose he decides to reward her financially in appreciation of her sharing part of her life with him. What combination of salaries and gifts is advantageous to both? And how much salary can he pay her legitimately without her having to pay income tax?

If she is single, he can pay her $2,950 per year, according to the 1977 tax revision, and she will not have to pay any federal income tax. However, each state has its own tax laws, so he will have to check this with his accountant.

On that $2,950 she must also pay social security, which is approximately six percent, and he must do the same (or he pays the whole 12 percent).

Suppose he is willing to give her more. The best way to handle this is to give her $3000 per year, on which there is no gift tax. In sum, he can pay and give her a total of $5950 a year and pay the rest of her expenses with no tax on the transaction.

Finally, let's look at an inconsistency in the law. Suppose I own an apartment building and have a female manager. I give her rent-free use of an apartment, and I pay her telephone and utility bills. She must declare all these as income for tax purposes. But if I am living with a woman who works for me for a salary and gets $3000 per year in gifts, and too, lives rent-free in an apartment I own, with her telephone and utility bills paid by me, she may not have to pay taxes on these.

The IRS is working at cross-purposes here. It penalizes the woman who is just earning a living while encouraging the woman who is "living in sin."

27

A Lesson from the Lee Marvin Case

The gist of an Associated Press release (San Francisco, December 27, 1976) is that a verbal agreement between unmarried couples to share property while living together can be valid and binding, according to the California Supreme Court in a case involving actor Lee Marvin.

In an appeal filed by Michelle Marvin she contended they verbally agreed in October 1964 to share earnings while living together. Miss Marvin, who changed her name legally from Michelle Triolla, contended she agreed to abandon her singing career for full-time homemaking in return for his promise to support her. They acted as husband and wife for six years.

She argued she was entitled to half the property acquired during their nonmarital relationship, including motion-picture rights worth more than $1 million.

"The fact that a man and a woman live together without marriage, and engage in a sexual relationship, does not in itself invalidate agreements between them relating to their earnings, property, or expenses," the decision said, reversing a lower-court ruling in favor of Lee Marvin. The woman's complaint, according to the higher court, stated a cause of action for breach of an express contract, although the contract was verbal. (This means she has a valid case, which she can try to win.)

"The courts may inquire into the conduct of the parties to determine whether that conduct demonstrates an implied contract or implied agreement of partnership or joint venture, or some other tacit understanding between the parties," the decision held.

The higher court also found that a nonmarital partner may recover funds for a "reasonable value of household services rendered, less the reasonable value of support received, if he can show he rendered services with the expectation of monetary reward."

Michelle Marvin would have had a stronger case if she had produced a written contract. My advice to every woman is: For God's sake, protect yourself. You can enjoy romance without blind trust. There is the old adage, "Marriage kills the romance," but cohabitation can have the same effect. If you're going to live with a man and you're going to do services for him, whether they are sexual or otherwise, put it in writing. Together you can write a contract stipulating each partner's duties and responsibilities. If any woman lived with me for six years and we loved each other, she would be entitled to more than a woman who was married to me for a few months and made me miserable.

With a written contract there is no need to substantiate that there were verbal promises. The contract can set forth the woman's duties and her compensation for performing them. Just as many clergymen have housekeepers who are under contract, Michelle Marvin would have been under contract to Lee Marvin for housekeeping duties. And as long as there is nothing illegal in the contract, it can be enforced.

The future will probably see more contracts between unmarried people who live together. There may come a time when state legislatures repeal their laws of cohabitation. Then people living together will be able to contract as partners according to their needs and relative financial positions.

PART FIVE

State-by-State Data

28

Explanation and Comments

Many of the terms used in the next chapter are self-explanatory. Others are treated at length throughout this book (the respective passages can be found through the index and the table of contents). Also see the following explanations.

adultery: Sexual relationship of a married person with someone other than his or her spouse. It requires, in legal definition, "penetration of the female organ by the male organ."

common-law marriage: Fifteen states and the District of Columbia recognize common-law marriage as a consequence of a man and a woman living together as husband and wife even though no marriage was solemnized by civil authority. The reasoning is that such couples consider themselves married and act as though they were married and therefore should be considered legally married; and only after a divorce can either spouse remarry. Seven other states recognize common-law marriage only if the sexual relationship began in another state where common-law marriage is valid. A very complex subject.

crime against nature: Sodomy, buggery.

dissolution of marriage: Term used now in several states instead of "divorce," also instead of "separation."

holographic will:　Handwritten will.

indignities:　Catch-all category for insulting, humiliating behavior.

malformation (*preventing intercourse*)*:*　Physical impairment of sex organs.

nonage:　Age younger than that required for marriage.

pregnancy:　Usually means pregnancy by another man before marriage unknown to the husband.

prostitution:　On the part of the wife only. (After the E.R.A. is passed, this law might be applicable to men, too.)

residence requirement:　The length of time one or both parties in a divorce action must have lived in the state where the suit is brought.

solemnized by proper authority, not:　Marriage performed by a person (for example, a public servant or a minister) who was not authorized by the state to do so.

vagrancy:　On the part of the husband only. (After the E.R.A. is passed, this law might be applicable to women, too.)

Note that each state has its own terminology and that these are the terms that are used in the next chapter. Two or more terms often have the same or a very similar meaning; for example, abandonment and desertion, alcoholism and drunkenness, insanity and mental incompetence, physical cruelty, violence, force, and duress.

29

State-by-State Data on Marriage and Divorce (The 50 States, the District of Columbia, Puerto Rico)

Alabama

Marriage
Minimum age: male, 17; female, 14
Age requiring parental consent: male, under 18; unless previously married; female, under 18 unless previously married
Age not requiring parental consent: male, 21; female, 18
Blood-test requirement: yes
Waiting period: none
Recognition of common-law marriage: yes
Grounds for divorce
Adultery
Habitual drunkenness or drug addiction
Imprisonment in penitentiary
Incapacity or impotence
Incompatibility
Insanity
Pregnancy (see page 128)
Separation without support
Violence and reasonable apprehension thereof
Voluntary abandonment

Where there has been a final judgment of divorce
from bed and board or of separate maintenance
(more than 2 years)

Grounds for legal separation
See grounds for divorce.

Grounds for annulment
Duress
Fraud, misrepresentation, or imposition
Mental incapacity
Mistake
Physical disease or incapacity
Pregnancy at time of marriage
Prior existing marriage

Residence requirement
6 months—if defendant is a nonresident (A wife
seeking divorce for nonsupport must have resided
in the state for 2 years and must have been
separated from her husband during this time.)

What happens with inheritance if there is no will
(intestacy)?

Real estate: The real estate of persons dying intestate
as to real estate descends, subject to the payment of
debts, charges against the estate, and the widow's
dower, as follows:

1. To the children of the intestate, or their descendants,
in equal parts.

2. If there are no children or their descendants, then
to the father and mother, in equal parts.

3. If there are no children or their descendants, and
if there be but one surviving parent, then one half
to such surviving parent, and the other half to the
brothers and sisters of the intestate, or their descendants, in equal parts.

4. If there are no children or their descendants, no
brothers or sisters or their descendants, and if there
be but one surviving parent, then the whole to such
surviving parent.

5. If there are no children or their descendants, no
father or mother, and no brothers or sisters or
their descendants, then the whole to the husband or
wife of the intestate.

6. If there are no children or their descendants, no father or mother, no brothers or sisters or their descendants, and no husband or wife, then to the next of kin to the intestate, in equal parts.

7. If there are no children or their descendants, no father or mother, no brothers or sisters or their descendants, no husband or wife, and no next of kin to the intestate, then to the next of kin of the intestate's predeceased spouse in the same order of priority as provided for descent to the kin of the intestate.

8. If there are no children or their descendants, no father or mother, no brothers or sisters or their descendants, no husband or wife, and no kin capable of inheriting, then the property falls to the state.

Personal estate: The personal estate of persons dying intestate as to personal estate, after the payment of debts and charges against the estate, is to be distributed in the same manner as his real estate, and according to the same rules; except that a widow, if there are no children, is entitled to all the personal estate; if there is only one child, is entitled to one-half; if more than one, and not more than four children, to an amount equal to a child's part; and if more than four children, to one-fifth.

Other questions

Are holographic wills recognized? No

Can support (separate maintenance) for wife and children be awarded from the time of filing for divorce until award of the final decree? Yes. (A wife may sue for alimony without suing for divorce.)

Can alimony be awarded to take effect after the final decree? Yes

Can custody be awarded with the divorce (dissolution) decree? Yes

Can child support be awarded with the divorce (dissolution) decree? Yes

Are there dower rights? Yes. (Divorce bars dower.)

Can property be divided and awarded with the divorce (dissolution) decree? Yes

Is this a community property state? No

Can court allow wife to resume her former name? No

Is there a uniform reciprocal enforcement-of-support act? Yes

Legal Referral Service

Birmingham, AL 35203: 900 Jefferson County Court House; 205-251-8006

Mobile, AL 36602: 6 St. Emanuel Street; 205-438-4381

Legal Aid

Birmingham, AL: G. Bennett Haynes, Jr., Legal Assistant Corporation of Birmingham

Mobile, AL 36602: Committee on Legal Aid, Mobile Bar Associates, New Court House Building; 205-438-4381

Armed Forces Legal Assistance

Army: Staff Judge Advocate, Hg 121st US ARCOM, 3620 8th Avenue, S, Birmingham, AL 35222

Navy: Legal Assistance Officer, Naval Legal Service Office Naval Base, Charleston, SC 29408

Air Force: Legal Assistance Office (JA), Craig AFB, AL 36701

Coast Guard: None

Legal Assistance for Service Men Committee: Alabama State Bar, P.O. Box 2106, Montgomery, AL 36103

Alaska

Marriage

Minimum age: male, 16; female, 16

Age requiring parental consent: male, under 18; female, under 18

Age not requiring parental consent: male, 18; female, 18

Blood-test requirement: yes

Waiting period: 3 days

Recognition of common-law marriage: no

Grounds for divorce
 Adultery
 Alcoholism (1 year)
 Cruelty, mental
 Cruelty, physical (personal indignities)
 Desertion, willful (1 year)
 Drug addiction
 Failure to consummate at time of marriage and continuing
 Felony conviction
 Incompatibility
 Insanity, postmarital (18 months)

Grounds for annulment
 Bigamy (marriage is "void")
 Blood relationship (marriage is "void")
 Force or duress
 Fraud
 Mental incompetence at time of marriage
 Nonage

Residence requirement
 None

What happens with inheritance if there is no will (intestacy)?

1. If there are no surviving parents or children of deceased, surviving spouse inherits the entire estate.
2. If there are no surviving children but parents of deceased are living, spouse inherits up to $50,000 plus one-half of the balance of the estate.
3. If there are children of the surviving spouse, spouse inherits the first $50,000 plus one-half of the balance of the estate.
4. If there are children, one or more of whom are not issue of the surviving spouse, spouse inherits one-half of the estate.

Other questions
 Are holographic wills recognized? Yes
 Can support (separate maintenance) for wife and children be awarded from the time of filing for divorce until award of the final decree? Yes
 Can alimony be awarded to take effect after the final decree? Yes

Can custody be awarded with the divorce (dissolution) decree? Yes

Can child support be awarded with the divorce (dissolution) decree? Yes

Are there dower rights? No

Can property be divided and awarded with the divorce (dissolution) decree? Yes

Is this a community property state? No

Can court allow wife to resume her former name? Yes

Is there a uniform reciprocal enforcement-of-support act? Yes

Legal Referral Service

Anchorage, AK 95510: 941 West 4th Avenue; 907-272-0352

Legal Aid

Anchorage, AK 95510: Alaska Legal Services Corporation, 524 West 6th Avenue; 907-272-9431

Armed Forces Legal Assistance

Army: Legal Assistance Office (SJA), Fort Wainwright, APO Seattle, WA 98731

Navy: Legal Assistance Officer, Naval Station (ADAK), FPO Seattle, WA 98791; 907-579-2257

Air Force: Legal Assistance Office, Elmendorf AFB, APO Seattle, WA 98742

Coast Guard: Legal Assistance Office, c/o Commander 17th Coast Guard District, FPO Seattle, WA 98771; 907-586-7298

Arizona

Marriage

Minimum age: male, 16; female, 16 (under 16 with parental and superior court consent)

Age requiring parental consent: male, under 18; female, under 18

Age not requiring parental consent: male, 18; female, 18

Blood-test requirement: yes (but can be waived)

Waiting period: none

Recognition of common-law marriage: no (unless created in another state)

Grounds for dissolution of marriage (divorce)

No-fault (irretrievable breakdown)

Grounds for legal separation

Irretrievable breakdown

Grounds for annulment

Marriage may be annulled if a condition exists that makes the marriage void.

Grounds for declaring the marriage void

Blood relationship

Residence requirement

Dissolution: 90 days (one spouse). Separation: One party must be domiciled in the state at the time action is begun.

What happens with inheritance if there is no will (intestacy)?

1. If there are no children of deceased, surviving spouse inherits the entire estate.

2. Regarding the intestate estate, both the decedent's separate property and the one-half of community property that belonged to decedent, the following passes to surviving spouse: (a) If there is no surviving issue or if there are surviving issue all of whom are issue of the surviving spouse also, the entire intestate estate. (b) If there are surviving issue one or more of whom are not issue of surviving spouse, one-half of the intestate separate property and no interest in the one-half of the community property which belonged to decedent.

Other questions

Are holographic wills recognized? Yes

Can support (separate maintenance) for wife and children be awarded from the time of filing for divorce until award of the final decree? Yes

Can alimony (called "spousal maintenance" in this state) be awarded to take effect after the final decree? Yes

Can custody be awarded with the divorce (dissolution) decree? Yes

Can child support be awarded with the divorce (dissolution) decree? Yes

Are there dower rights? No

Can property be divided and awarded with the divorce (dissolution) decree? Yes

Is this a community property state? Yes

Can court allow wife to resume her former name? Yes.

Is there a uniform reciprocal enforcement-of-support act? Yes

Legal Referral Service

Phoenix, AZ 85102: 3033 North Central Avenue, Suite 107; 602-277-5753

Tucson, AZ 85701: 201 North Stone Avenue, Suite 218; 602-623-4625

Legal Aid

Phoenix, AZ 85025: Federal Public Defender, District of Arizona, U.S. District Court; 602-261-3561

Tucson, AZ 85701: County Bar Association, 55 West Congress Street; 602-623-6260

Armed Forces Legal Assistance

Army: Legal Assistance Office, YUMA Proving Ground, P.O. Box 3023, Yuma, AZ 85364. Legal Assistance Office (SJA), Fort Huachuca, AZ 85613

Navy: Legal Assistance Officer, Naval Legal Service Office, Naval Station, San Diego, CA 92136; 714-235-1612

Air Force: Legal Assistant Office, Davis-Monthan AFB, AZ 85707; 602-793-5241

Coast Guard: None

Arkansas

Marriage

Minimum age: male, 17; female, 16 (under this age with court and parental consent. In case of pregnancy, probate court may grant license.)

Age requiring parental consent: male, under 18; female, under 18

Age not requiring parental consent: male, 18; female, 18

Blood-test requirement: yes

Waiting period: 3 days

Recognition of common-law marriage: no (unless created in another state)

Grounds for divorce

Adultery

Alcoholism (1 year)

Bigamy

Cruelty, mental (personal indignities)

- Cruelty, physical (treatment endangering life)

Desertion (1 year)

Felony conviction

Impotence at time of marriage

Insanity, postmarital (confinement for 3 years)

No-fault (separated for 3 years)

Nonsupport

Separation for 3 years

Grounds for annulment

Force or duress

Fraud

Impotence at time of marriage

Malformation preventing intercourse

Mental incompetence at marriage

Nonage

Sterility

Grounds for declaring the marriage void

Blood relationship

Nonage

Note: After 5 years abandonment and presumption of death, abandoned spouse may remarry.

Residence requirement

60 days before taking action

What happens with inheritance if there is no will (intestacy)?

If spouse has not waived her dower rights, if there are no descendants and the marriage existed continuously for 3 years before death, surviving spouse inherits all; if continuously married less than 3 years before death, spouse inherits one-half.

Other questions

Are holographic wills recognized? Yes. (Three disinterested witnesses are required to verify handwriting and signature.)

Can support (separate maintenance) for wife and children be awarded from the time of filing for divorce until award of the final decree? Yes

Can alimony be awarded to take effect after the final decree? Yes

Can custody be awarded with the divorce (dissolution) decree? Yes

Can child support be awarded with the divorce (dissolution) decree? Yes

Are there dower rights? Yes

Can property be divided and awarded with the divorce (dissolution) decree? Upon her divorce, wife is entitled to one-third of husband's personal property and one-third of his lands for life.

Is this a community property state? No

Can court allow the wife to resume her former name? Yes (if there were no children born of the marriage)

Is there a uniform reciprocal enforcement-of-support act? Yes

Legal Referral Service

Little Rock, AR 72201: State Wide Legal Referral Service, 400 West Markham Street; 800-482-9406

Legal Aid

Little Rock, AR 72201: Public Defender, 6th Judicial District, Pulaski County Court House; 501-374-9203

Armed Forces Legal Assistance

Army: Legal Assistance Office, Office of the Post Judge Advocate, U.S. Army Pine Bluff Arsenal, Pine Bluff, AR 71601

Navy: Legal Assistance Office, Headquarters 8th Naval District, New Orleans, LA 70140; 504-366-2311, ext. 414

Air Force: Legal Assistance Office (JA), Little Rock
   AFB, AR 72076
Coast Guard: None

California

Marriage
   Minimum age: no minimum age with parental and
      court consent
   Age requiring parental consent: male, under 18;
      female, under 18
   Age not requiring parental consent: male, 18; fe-
      male, 18
   Blood-test requirement: yes
   Waiting period: none
   Recognition of common-law marriage: no (unless
      created in another state)
Grounds for dissolution of marriage and legal separation
   Incurable insanity (obligation to support insane
      spouse is not removed with decree of dissolution)
   No-fault (irreconcilable differences)
Grounds for legal separation
   Either party can request a legal separation using
      the grounds above. The court can grant a legal
      separation if both parties consent or if one does
      not appear.
Grounds for judgment of nullity (annulment)
   Bigamy (marriage is "void")
   Blood relationship (marriage is "void")
   Force or duress
   Fraud
   Impotence undisclosed at marriage
   Insanity at marriage (mental incompetence)
   Malformation preventing intercourse
   Nonage
   Sterility undisclosed at marriage
Residence requirement
   One party must be resident of the state for 6 months,
      and resident of county where the suit is filed for
      3 months.

What happens with inheritance if there is no will (intestacy)?

Surviving spouse inherits one-third of the separate property if there is more than one child, and one-half of the separate property if there is one child or if there are other relatives specified by California law. Spouse inherits entire estate if there are no children or aforementioned relatives. Surviving spouse is entitled to all the community property whether or not there are children.

Other questions

Are holographic wills recognized? Yes

Can support (separate maintenance) for wife and children be awarded from the time of filing for divorce until award of the final decree? Yes

Can alimony be awarded to take effect after the final decree? Yes

Can custody be awarded with the divorce (dissolution) decree? Yes

Can child support be awarded with the divorce (dissolution) decree? Yes

Are there dower rights? No

Can property be divided and awarded with the divorce (dissolution) decree? Yes

Is this a community property state? Yes

Can court allow wife to resume her former name? Yes

Is there a uniform reciprocal enforcement-of-support act? Yes

Legal Referral Service

Los Angeles, CA 90045: 8820 South Sepulveda Boulevard, Suite 107; 213-645-6078

Sacramento, CA 95814: 901 H Street, Suite 101; 916-444-2333

San Diego, CA 92101: 1200 3d Avenue, Suite 412; 714-231-8581

San Francisco, CA 94104: 220 Bush Street, 21st Floor; 415-391-6102

Legal Aid

Los Angeles, CA 90005: ACLU Foundation of

Southern California, 633 South Shatto Place; 213-487-1720

Sacramento, CA 95814: California Rural Legal Assistance Branch, 1900 K Street, Suite 203; 916-446-7901

San Diego, CA 92101: Legal Aid Society of San Diego, 400 Granger Building, 964 5th Avenue; 714-232-2214

San Francisco, CA 94110: Mission Community Legal Defense, 2922 Mission Street; 415-826-5333

Armed Forces Legal Assistance

Army: Legal Assistance Officer, Office of the Staff Judge Advocate, CDCEC, Fort Ord, CA 93941. Staff Judge Advocate, Headquarters 6th Army, Presidio of San Francisco, CA 94129

Navy: Legal Assistance Office, Naval Legal Service Office, Naval Station, P.O. Box 138, Building 224, San Diego, CA 92136; 714-235-1612

Air Force: Legal Assistance Office (JA), Travis AFB, CA 94535; 707-738-4011. Legal Assistance Office (JA), McClellan AFB, CA 95652; 916-643-2111

Coast Guard: Commanding Officer, U.S. Coast Guard Training Center, Government Island, Alameda, CA 94501; 415-273-7585, 415-536-7585, 415-465-8529

Colorado

Marriage

Minimum age: male, none; female, none

Age requiring parental consent: male, under 16 (with court consent); female, under 18 (under 16 with court consent)

Age not requiring parental consent: male, 18; female, 18

Blood-test requirement: yes

Waiting period: none

Recognition of common-law marriage: still recognized despite passage of the Uniform Marriage Act

Grounds for divorce

No-fault (irretrievable breakdown)

Grounds for legal separation

No-fault (irretrievable breakdown). The decree is granted if one party so requests and the other does not object. Conversion to dissolution of marriage is made after 6 months, on motion of either party.

Grounds for declaration of invalidity

Duress

Fraud

Impotence at time of marriage

Malformation preventing intercourse

Marriage as a jest or dare

Marriage prohibited by law, such as bigamy or blood relationship

Mental incompetence at time of marriage

Nonage

Residence requirement

90 days (one party)

What happens with inheritance if there is no will (intestacy)?

If there are no surviving children of deceased, surviving spouse inherits the entire estate. If there are children of the surviving spouse, spouse inherits up to $25,000 and one-half of the balance of the estate. If there are children, one or more of whom are not issue of the surviving spouse, spouse inherits one-half of the estate.

Other questions

Are holographic wills recognized? Yes

Can support (separate maintenance) for wife and children be awarded from the time of filing for divorce until award of the final decree? Yes

Can alimony be awarded to take effect after the final decree? Yes

Can custody be awarded with the divorce (dissolution) decree? Yes

Can child support be awarded with the divorce (dissolution) decree? Yes

Are there dower rights? No

Can property be divided and awarded with the divorce (dissolution) decree? Yes

Is this a community property state? No

Can court allow wife to resume her former name? Yes

Is there a uniform reciprocal enforcement-of-support act? Yes

Legal Referral Service

Denver, CO 80204: 1117 Cherokee Street; 303-573-8871

Legal Aid

Denver, CO 80205: Colorado Legal Aid Society Services, 912 Broadway Street

Armed Forces Legal Assistance

Army: Legal Assistance Officer, (SJA), Fitzsimmons General Hospital, Denver, CO 80240

Navy: Legal Assistance Officer, Naval Legal Service Office, Naval Training Center, Great Lakes, IL 60088; 312-688-3340

Air Force: Staff Judge Advocate, Room 244, Harmon Hall, USAF Academy, Colorado Springs, CO 80840

Coast Guard: None

Connecticut

Marriage

Minimum age: male, 16; female, 16

Age requiring parental consent: male, under 18; female, under 18

Age not requiring parental consent: male, 18; female, 18

Blood-test requirement: yes

Waiting period: 4 days

Recognition of common-law marriage: no

Grounds for dissolution of marriage (divorce)

Adultery

Alcoholism

Cruelty, mental (intolerable)

Cruelty, physical (intolerable)

Desertion (1 year)

Felony conviction (with imprisonment of more than 1 year)

Fraud

Imprisonment (more than 1 year)

No-fault (irretrievable breakdown: separated for 18 months continuously due to incompatibility with no reasonable prospect of reconciliation)

Grounds for legal separation

See grounds for dissolution of marriage.

Grounds for annulment

Blood relationship

Conviction in court of an offense against chastity

Grounds for declaring the marriage void

Blood relationship

Residence requirement

1 year

What happens with inheritance if there is no will (intestacy)?

If there are no surviving children, spouse inherits the entire estate. If there are children, spouse inherits up to $50,000 and one-half of the remaining estate.

Other questions

Are holographic wills recognized? No (unless created in another state)

Can support (separate maintenance) for wife and children be awarded from the time of filing for divorce until award of the final decree? Yes

Can alimony be awarded to take effect after the final decree? Yes

Can custody be awarded with the divorce (dissolution) decree? Yes

Can child support be awarded with the divorce (dissolution) decree? Yes

Are there dower rights? Yes

Can property be divided and awarded with the divorce (dissolution) decree? Yes

Is this a community property state? No

Can court allow wife to resume her former name? Yes

Is there a uniform reciprocal enforcement-of-support act? Yes

Legal Referral Service

Hartford, CT 06103: 266 Pearl Street; 203-525-6052

Legal Aid

Hartford, CT 06103: Louis Roberts, Public Defender, 16th Circuit, 750 Main Street

Armed Forces Legal Assistance

Army: None

Navy: Legal Assistance Officer, Naval Legal Service Branch Office, Naval Submarine Base, Groton, CT 06340; 203-449-3751

Air Force: None

Coast Guard: Legal Assistance Officer, U.S. Coast Guard Academy, New London, CT 06320; 230-443-8463

Delaware

Marriage

Minimum age: male, 18; female, 16

Age requiring parental consent: male, under 18 cannot marry; female, under 18

Age not requiring parental consent: male, 18; female, 18

Blood-test requirement: yes

Waiting period: 1 day for residents; 4 days for nonresidents

Recognition of common-law marriage: no (unless created in another state)

Grounds for divorce

No-fault (irretrievable breakdown)

Grounds for annulment

Blood relationship

Duress

Fraud

Incapacity, mental
Incapacity, physical
Nonage

Grounds for voiding and prohibiting a marriage
Blood relationship

Grounds for making a marriage voidable
Alcoholism
Drug abuse
Paupers (marriage between)
Probation or parole (need written consent from the chief officer)
Unsoundness of mind of any degree
Venereal or other communicable disease unknown to the other party

Residence requirement
3 months

What happens with inheritance if there is no will (intestacy)?

1. If there are no surviving children or parents of decedent, spouse takes the entire estate.
2. If decedent is survived by issue or a parent, spouse takes the first $50,000 of the intestate personal estate, and one-half of the balance of the personal estate and a life estate in the intestate real estate.
3. If there is surviving issue which is not issue of the surviving spouse, then surviving spouse takes one-half of the intestate personal property and a life interest in the intestate real property.

Other questions
Are holographic wills recognized? Yes
Can support (separate maintenance) for wife and children be awarded from the time of filing for divorce until award of the final decree? Yes
Can alimony be awarded to take effect after the final decree? Yes
Can custody be awarded with the divorce (dissolution) decree? Yes
Can child support be awarded with the divorce (dissolution) decree? Yes
Are there dower rights? No

Can property be divided and awarded with the divorce (dissolution) decree? Yes

Is this a community property state? No

Can court allow wife to resume her formal name? Yes

Is there a uniform reciprocal enforcement-of-support act? Yes

Legal Referral Service

Wilmington DE 19801: 920 Market Tower; 302-658-5278

Legal Aid

Wilmington, DE 19801: Community Legal Aid Society, 204 West 7th Street; 302-665-7351

Armed Forces Legal Assistance

Army: None

Navy: Legal Assistance Officer, Naval Legal Service Office, Naval Base, Philadelphia, PA 19112

Air Force: Legal Assistance Officer, Dover AFB, DE 19901

Coast Guard: None

Armed Forces Committee: Delaware State Bar Association, 4072 Du Pont Building, Wilmington, DE 19801

Florida

Marriage

Minimum age: male, 18; female, 16 (younger if she has or is expecting a child)

Age requiring parental consent: male, under 21; female, under 18

Age not requiring parental consent: male, 21; female, 21

Blood-test requirement: yes

Waiting period: 3 days

Recognition of common-law marriage: no

Grounds for dissolution of marriage (divorce)

No-fault (irretrievable breakdown)

Grounds for annulment

At its discretion, the court can grant annulment

for fraud, duress, or other recognized legal causes.

The spouse not seeking dissolution or annulment can ask the court for alimony and child support.

Residence requirement
6 months

What happens with inheritance if there is no will (intestacy)?

If there are no children, surviving spouse inherits the entire estate. If there are children, spouse inherits the first $20,000 and one-half of the balance of the estate. If any of the children are not those of surviving spouse, spouse inherits one-half of the estate.

Other questions

Are holographic wills recognized? No

Can support (separate maintenance) for wife and children be awarded from the time of filing for divorce until award of the final decree? Yes

Can alimony be awarded to take effect after the final decree? Yes (to either party)

Can custody be awarded with the divorce (dissolution) decree? Yes

Can child support be awarded with the divorce (dissolution) decree? Yes

Are there dower rights? No

Can property be divided and awarded with the divorce (dissolution) decree? Yes

Is this a community property state? No

Can court allow wife to resume her former name? Yes

Is there a uniform reciprocal enforcement-of-support act? Yes

Legal Referral Service
Tallahassee, FL 32304: Florida Bar; 904-222-5286, 800-342-8011 (in-state WATS line)

Legal Aid
Tallahassee, FL 32301: Leon County Legal Aid Society, 103B, Leon County Courthouse

Armed Force Legal Assistance
Army: Office of the Staff Judge Advocate, HQ U.S.

Readiness Command, MacDill AFB, FL 33608
Navy: Legal Assistance Officer, Naval Air Station, Cecil Field, Jacksonville, FL 32215; 904-434-1730
Air Force: Legal Assistance Office (JA), MacDill AFB, FL 33608; 813-830-4421
Coast Guard: Legal Assistance Officer, c/o Commander 7th Coast Guard District, Federal Building 51 Southwest 1st Avenue, Miami, FL 33130; 305-350-5653

Georgia

Marriage
Minimum age: male, 18; female, 16 (If either is under age, parents' consent and doctor's certificate that she is pregnant are required.)
Age requiring parental consent: male, under 18 cannot marry; female, under 18
Age not requiring parental consent: male, 18; female, 18
Blood-test requirement: yes
Waiting period: 3 days
Recognition of common-law marriage: yes
Grounds for divorce
Adultery
Alcoholism (habitual intoxication)
Blood relationship
Conviction for moral turpitude (2 years or more)
Cruelty, mental
Cruelty, physical
Desertion (1 year)
Drug addiction
Duress or force
Fraud
Impotence at time of marriage
Mental incompetence at time of marriage
Mental illness, postmarital (2 years)
No-fault (irretrievable breakdown)
Pregnancy (see page 128)

Grounds for legal separation
  Bigamy
  Blood relationship
  Duress or force
  Fraud
  Insanity at time of marriage
Grounds for annulment
  Bigamy
  Blood relationship
  Nonage
Grounds for voiding a marriage
  Bigamy
  Blood relationship
  Duress
  Fraud
  Mental incompetence at time of marriage
Residence requirement
  6 months

What happens with inheritance if there is no will (intestacy)?
If there are no children, surviving spouse inherits the entire estate. If there are children, spouse shares equally with them, unless there are more than five children.
  If so, spouse inherits only one-fifth of the estate.
Other questions
  Are holographic wills recognized? No
  Can support (separate maintenance) for wife and children be awarded from the time of filing for divorce until award of the final decree? Yes
  Can alimony be awarded to take effect after the final decree? Yes
  Can custody be awarded with the divorce (dissolution) decree? Yes
  Can child support be awarded with the divorce (dissolution) decree? Yes
  Are there dower rights? No
  Can property be divided and awarded with the divorce (dissolution) decree? Yes
  Is this a community property state? No
  Can court allow wife to resume her former name? Yes

Is there a uniform reciprocal enforcement-of-support act? Yes (with modifications)

Legal Referral Service
Atlanta, GA 30303: 55 Marietta Street, NW; 800-282-5851

Legal Aid
Atlanta, GA 30303: Atlanta Legal Aid Society, 153 Pryor Street, SW; 404-524-5811

Armed Forces Legal Assistance
Army: Legal Assistance Officer, Soldier Advocate Division, U.S. Army Infantry Center, Fort Benning, GA 31905

Navy: Legal Assistance Officer, Naval Legal Service Office, Naval Base, Charleston, SC 29408; 803-743-4740

Air Force: Legal Assistance Office (JA), Moody AFB, GA 31601

Coast Guard: None

Hawaii

Marriage
Minimum age: male, 16; female, 16 (either: 15 with court permission)

Age requiring parental consent: male, under 18; female, under 18

Age not requiring parental consent: male, 18; female, 18

Blood-test requirement: yes

Waiting period: none

Recognition of common-law marriage: no

Grounds for divorce
No-fault (irretrievable breakdown)
Separation (2 years)

Grounds for legal separation
No-fault (irretrievable breakdown)
Separation (2 years)

Grounds for annulment
Bigamy

Blood relationship
Duress
Fraud
Impotence
Insanity
Loathsome disease concealed from other party
Nonage (either party)

Grounds for declaring the marriage void
See grounds for annulment.

Residence requirement
3 months. But at least one party must have been domiciled or physically present within the state for a continuous period of 1 year next preceding the application.

What happens with inheritance if there is no will (intestacy)?

1. If there are no surviving parents or children of deceased, surviving spouse inherits the entire estate.
2. If there are no surviving children but parents of deceased are living, the remaining spouse inherits one-half of the balance of the estate.
3. If there are children of surviving spouse, spouse inherits one-half of the balance of the estate.

Other questions
Are holographic wills recognized? No
Can support (separate maintenance) for wife and children be awarded from the time of filing for divorce until award of the final decree? Yes
Can alimony be awarded to take effect after the final decree? Yes
Can custody be awarded with the divorce (dissolution) decree? Yes
Can child support be awarded with the divorce (dissolution) decree? Yes
Are there dower rights? Yes (in property owned before July 1, 1977)
Can property be divided and awarded with the divorce (dissolution) decree? Yes
Is this a community property state? No
Can court allow wife to resume her former name? Yes

Is there a uniform reciprocal enforcement-of-support act? Yes

Legal Referral Service

Honolulu, HI 96810: Lawyer Referral Service, Marie Matsuda Hong, P.O. Box 26; 808-537-9140

Legal Aid

Honolulu, HI 96817: Legal Aid Society of Hawaii, Suite 404, 200 North Vineyard Boulevard; 808-536-4302

Armed Forces Legal Assistance

Army: Legal Assistance Office, U.S.A. Support Command, Hawaii, APO San Francisco, CA 96557

Navy: Legal Assistance Officer, Naval Legal Service Office, Naval Station Pearl Harbor, FPO San Francisco, CA 96610

Air Force: Legal Assistance Office, (JA), 15 Air Base Wing, Hickam AFB, APO San Francisco, CA 96553

Coast Guard: Legal Assistance Officer, c/o Commander 14th Coast Guard District, 677 ALA Moana, Honolulu, HI 96813; 808-546-7110

Idaho

Marriage

Minimum age: male, 16; female, 14

Age requiring parental consent: male, under 18; female, under 16

Age not requiring parental consent: male, 18; female, 18

Blood-test requirement: yes

Waiting period: 3 days if under 18

Recognition of common-law marriage: yes

Grounds for divorce

Adultery

Alcoholism

Cruelty

Desertion

Felony conviction
Insanity
Neglect
No-fault (irreconcilable differences)
Separation (5 years)

Grounds for legal separation

Idaho does not recognize legal separation but does recognize the right to separate maintenance.

Grounds for annulment

Bigamy
Duress
Fraud
Impotence
Insanity
Nonage

Grounds for declaring the marriage void

Bigamy
Blood relationship

Residence requirement

6 weeks

What happens with inheritance if there is no will (intestacy)?

1. If there are no surviving parents or children of deceased, surviving spouse inherits the entire estate.
2. If there are no surviving children but parents of deceased are living, the remaining spouse inherits $50,000 and one-half of the balance of the estate.
3. If there are children of surviving spouse, spouse inherits the first $50,000 and one-half of the balance of the estate.
4. If there are children one or more of whom are not issue of surviving spouse, spouse inherits one-half of the estate.
5. Because this is a community property state, the above four provisions apply only to the separate properties of the deceased.

Other questions

Are holographic wills recognized? Yes

Can support (separate maintenance) for wife and children be awarded from the time of filing for divorce until award of the final decree? Yes

Can alimony be awarded to take effect after the final decree? Yes

Can custody be awarded with the divorce (dissolution) decree? Yes

Can child support be awarded with the divorce (dissolution) decree? Yes

Are there dower rights? No

Can property be divided and awarded with the divorce (dissolution) decree? Yes

Is this a community property state? Yes

Can court allow wife to resume her former name? Yes

Is there a uniform reciprocal enforcement-of-support act? Yes

Legal Referral Service

Boise, ID 83701: Lawyer Referral Service, Ronald L. Kull, Executive Director, P.O. Box 895; 208-342-8958

Legal Aid

Boise, ID 83701: Western Idaho Legal Aid Branch, 104½ South Capitol Boulevard; 208-345-0106

Armed Forces Legal Assistance

Army: None

Navy: Legal Assistance Office, Naval Legal Service Office, Seattle, WA 98115; 206-527-3835

Air Force: Legal Assistance Office (JA), Mountain Home AFB, ID 83648

Coast Guard: None

Illinois

Marriage

Minimum age: male, 16; female, 16

Age requiring parental consent: male, under 18; female, under 18

Age not requiring parental consent: male, 18; female, 18

Blood-test requirement: yes

Waiting period: 3 days (without court order)

Recognition of common-law marriage: no

Grounds for divorce
  Adultery
  Alcoholism (2 years)
  Attempt to murder spouse
  Bigamy
  Cruelty, mental (extreme and repeated)
  Cruelty, physical (extreme and repeated)
  Desertion (1 year)
  Drug addiction (2 years)
  Felony Conviction
  Impotence at time of marriage
  Venereal disease
Grounds for legal separation
  At discretion of judge
Grounds for annulment
  Blood relationship (at discretion of judge)
  Duress (at discretion of judge)
  Fraud (at discretion of judge)
  Incapacity, mental (at discretion of judge)
  Incapacity, physical (at discretion of judge)
  Nonage (at discretion of judge)
Grounds for declaring marriage invalid
  Blood relationship
  Prior undissolved marriage

Note: Separate maintenance (support) can be awarded "if court finds that without fault or provocation by petitioner other party has committed what would be ground for divorce."
Residence requirement
  90 days
What happens with inheritance if there is no will (intestacy)?
If there are no decendants, surviving spouse inherits the entire estate. If there are descendants, spouse inherits one-third of the estate.
Other questions
  Are holographic wills recognized? No
  Can support (separate maintenance) for wife and children be awarded from the time of filing for divorce until award of the final decree? Yes

Can alimony be awarded to take effect after the final decree? Yes

Can custody be awarded with the divorce (dissolution) decree? Yes

Can child support be awarded with the divorce (dissolution) decree? Yes

Are there dower rights? No

Can property be divided and awarded with the divorce (dissolution) decree? Yes

Is this a community property state? No

Can court allow wife to resume her former name? Yes

Is there a uniform reciprocal enforcement-of-support act? Yes

Legal Referral Service

Chicago, IL 60603: Lawyer Reference Plan, Chicago Bar Association, Terence M. Murphy, Director, 29 South LaSalle Street, Room 1040; 312-782-7438, ext. 253

Springfield, IL 62701: Lawyer Referral Service, Mary D. Smith, Referral Secretary, Illinois Bar Center; 800-252-8916 (WATS line)

Legal Aid

Chicago, IL 60601: Illinois Defender Project, Suite 1225, 180 North LaSalle Street; 312-263-0982

Springfield, IL 62701: Land of Lincoln Legal Assistance Foundation, 516 East Monroe Street; 217-544-7492

Armed Forces Legal Assistance

Army: Legal Assistance Officer, HQ U.S.A. Recruiting Command, Fort Sheridan, IL 60037

Navy: Legal Assistance Officer, Naval Legal Service Office, Naval Training Center, Great Lakes, IL 60088; 312-688-3340

Air Force: Legal Assistance Office (JA), Chanute AFB, IL 61868

Coast Guard: None

Indiana

Marriage
   Minimum age: male, 18; female, 16
   Age requiring parental consent: male, under 18 cannot marry; female, under 18
   Age not requiring parental consent: male, 18; female, 18
   Blood-test requirement: yes
   Waiting period: 3 days
   Recognition of common-law marriage: no
Grounds for dissolution of marriage
   Felony
   Impotence
   Insanity
Grounds for divorce
   No-fault (irretrievable breakdown)
Grounds for annulment
   Fraud
   Insanity
   Nonage
Grounds for declaring the marriage void
   Bigamy
   Blood relationship
Residence requirement
   6 months
What happens with inheritance if there is no will (intestacy)?
If there are no children, spouse inherits the entire estate. If there is one child, spouse inherits one-half. If there are two of more children, spouse inherits one-third.
Other questions
   Are holographic wills recognized? No
   Can support (separate maintenance) for wife and children be awarded from the time of filing for divorce until award of the final decree? Yes
   Can alimony be awarded to take effect after the final decree? No

Can custody be awarded with the divorce (dissolution) decree? Yes

Can child support be awarded with the divorce (dissolution) decree? Yes

Are there dower rights? No

Can property be divided and awarded with the divorce (dissolution) decree? Yes

Is this a community property state? No

Can court allow wife to resume her former name? Yes

Is there a uniform reciprocal enforcement-of-support act? Yes

Legal Referral Service

Indianapolis, IN 46204: Lawyer Referral Service, Indianapolis Bar Association, 1 Indiana Square, #2550; 317-632-8205

Legal Aid

Indianapolis, IN 46204: Indianapolis Legal Aid Society, Room 122, 615 North Alabama Street; 317-635-9538

Armed Forces Legal Assistance

Army: Legal Assistance Office, Post Judge Advocate, HQ, Fort Benjamin Harrison, IN 46216

Navy: Legal Assistance Officer, Naval Legal Service Office, Naval Training Center, Great Lakes, IL 60088; 312-688-3340

Air Force: Legal Assistance Office (JA), Grissom AFB, IN 46970; 317-689-2211, exts. 2231, 2232

Coast Guard: None

Legal Assistance for Service Men Committee: Evansville Bar Association, 1331 Division Street, Evansville, IN 47714

Iowa

Marriage

Minimum age: male, 16; female, 16

Age requiring parental consent: male, under 18; female, under 18

Age not requiring parental consent: male, 18; female, 18

Blood-test requirement: yes
Waiting period: 3 days
Recognition of common-law marriage: yes

Grounds for dissolution of marriage (divorce)
No-fault (breakdown of marriage relationship to the extent that the legitimate objects of matrimony have been destroyed and there remains no reasonable likelihood that the marriage can be preserved)

Grounds for legal separation
See grounds for dissolution of marriage.

Grounds for annulment
Impotence at time of marriage
Insanity at time of marriage (mental incapacity or mental retardation at time of marriage)
Marriage prohibited by law (see grounds for declaring the marriage void)

Grounds for declaring the marriage void
Bigamy
Blood relationship
Nonage (if declared before reaching the age of 18)

Residence requirement
None, if both partners are residents. One year if spouse being sued is a nonresident.

What happens with inheritance if there is no will (intestacy)?
If there are no children, spouse inherits the entire estate. If there are children, surviving spouse inherits one-third of the estate; if the estate is large enough, surviving spouse is guaranteed $25,000 even if it exceeds one-third.

Other questions
Are holographic wills recognized? No
Can support (separate maintenance) for wife and children be awarded from the time of filing for divorce until award of the final decree? Yes
Can alimony be awarded to take effect after the final decree? Yes
Can custody be awarded with the divorce (dissolution) decree? Yes
Can child support be awarded with the divorce (dissolution) decree? Yes

Are there dower rights? Common-law dower has been abolished, but a statutory scheme approximating dower does exist. Court cases have mentioned "dower" as recently as 1977.

Can property be divided and awarded with the divorce (dissolution) decree? Yes

Is this a community property state? No

Can court allow wife to resume her former name? Yes

Is there a uniform reciprocal enforcement-of-support act? Yes

Legal Referral Service

Des Moines, IA 50309: Lawyer Referral Service, Polk County Bar Association, 1101 Fleming Boulevard; 515-280-7429

Legal Aid

Des Moines, IA 50309: Legal Aid Society of Polk County, Iowa, 102 East Grand Avenue; 515-282-8375

Armed Forces Legal Assistance

Army: None

Navy: Legal Assistance Officer, Naval Legal Service Office, Naval Training Center, Great Lakes, IL. 60088; 312-688-3340

Air Force: None

Coast Guard: None

Military Law Committee: Iowa State Bar Association, 211 West Monroe Street, Mount Pleasant, IA 52641

Kansas

Marriage

Minimum age: male, 18; female, 18

Age requiring parental consent: male under 18 cannot marry; female, under 18 cannot marry

Age not requiring parental consent: male, 18; female, 18

Blood-test requirement: yes

Waiting period: 3 days

Recognition of common-law marriage: yes

Grounds for divorce
  Abandonment (desertion: 1 year)
  Adultery
  Alcoholism
  Cruelty, mental
  Cruelty, physical
  Felony conviction
  Imprisonment
  Incompatibility
  Insanity, postmarital (3 years)
  Neglect (gross)

Grounds for separate maintenance (legal separation)
  See grounds for divorce.

Grounds for annulment
  Bigamy
  Blood relationship
  Duress or force
  Fraud
  Impotence at time of marriage
  Insanity at time of marriage
  Pregnancy (see page 128)

Grounds for declaring the marriage void
  Blood relationship

Residence requirement
  60 days

What happens with inheritance if there is no will (intestacy)?

One-half to surviving spouse and one-half to children.
  Of course if there are no children, spouse inherits the entire estate.

Other questions
  Are holographic wills recognized? No
  Can support (separate maintenance) for wife and children be awarded from the time of filing for divorce until award of the final decree? Yes
  Can alimony be awarded to take effect after the final decree? Yes
  Can custody be awarded with the divorce (dissolution) decree? Yes

Can child support be awarded with the divorce (dissolution) decree? Yes

Are there dower rights? No

Can property be divided and awarded with the divorce (dissolution) decree? Yes

Is this a community property state? No

Can court allow wife to resume her former name? Yes

Is there a uniform reciprocal enforcement-of-support act? Yes

Legal Referral Service

Topeka, KS 66601: Lawyer Referral Service, Kansas Bar Association, P.O. Box 1037, 1334 Topeka Boulevard

Legal Aid

Kansas City, KS 66101: Wyandotte County Legal Aid Society, 909 Huron Building, 907 North Seventh Street; 913-621-0200

Armed Forces Legal Assistance

Army: Legal Assistance Officer, HQ U.S.A. Recruiting Command, Fort Sheridan, KS 60037

Navy: Legal Assistance Officer, Naval Legal Service Office, Naval Training Center, Great Lakes, IL. 60088; 312-688-3340

Air Force: Legal Assistance Office (JA), Chanute AFB, KS 61868

Coast Guard: None

Kentucky

Marriage

Minimum age: male, none; female, none (Either may legally apply for license with consent of one parent or if female is pregnant.)

Age requiring parental consent: male, under 18; female, under 18

Age not requiring consent: male, 18; female, 18

Blood-test requirement: yes

Waiting period: 3 days

Recognition of common-law marriage: no (unless created in another state)

Grounds for divorce

No-fault (irretrievable breakdown)

Grounds for declaring the marriage invalid

Alcoholism
Bigamy
Blood relationship
Drug taking
Fraud
Impotence
Insanity at time of marriage
Malformation preventing intercourse
Nonage
Not solemnized by proper authority
Pregnancy (see page 128)
Sterility

Grounds for declaring the marriage void

Bigamy
Blood relationship
Insanity at time of marriage
Nonage
Not solemnized by proper authority

Residence requirement

180 days

What happens with inheritance if there is no will (intestacy)?

If there are no children, spouse inherits the entire estate. If there are children, surviving spouse inherits one-third.

Other questions

Are holographic wills recognized? Yes

Can support (separate maintenance) for wife and children be awarded from the time of filing for divorce until award of the final decree? Yes

Can alimony be awarded to take effect after the final decree? Yes

Can custody be awarded with the divorce (dissolution) decree? Yes

Can child support be awarded with the divorce (dissolution) decree? Yes

Are there dower rights? Yes

Can property be divided and awarded with the divorce (dissolution) decree? Yes

Is this a community property state? No

Can court allow wife to resume her former name? Yes

Is there a uniform reciprocal enforcement-of-support act? Yes

Legal Referral Service

Lexington, KY 40505: Lawyer Referral Service, Fayette County Bar Association, 415 Parkview Avenue; 606-252-2809

Louisville, KY 40202: Lawyer Referral Service, Louisville Bar Association, 400 Court House; 520-583-5314

Legal Aid

Lexington, KY 40507: Fayette County Legal Aid, 180 Market Street; 606-255-8025

Louisville, KY 40402: Legal Aid Society of Louisville, 307 South 5th Street

Armed Forces Legal Assistance

Army: Legal Assistance Officer, HQ U.S. Army Armor Center, Fort Knox, KY 40121

Navy: Legal Assistance Officer, Naval Legal Service Office, Naval Base, Norfolk, VA 23511; 804-444-7561

Air Force: None

Coast Guard: None

Louisiana

Marriage

Minimum age: male, 18; female, 16

Age requiring parental consent: male, under 18 cannot marry; female, under 18

Age not requiring parental consent: male, 18; female, 18

Blood-test requirement: yes

Waiting period: 3 days

Recognition of common-law marriage: no

Grounds for divorce
  Adultery
  Felony conviction
  Imprisonment
  No-fault (separated 2 years)
Grounds for legal separation
  Abandonment
  Adultery
  Alcoholism
  Cruelty, mental
  Cruelty, physical
  Desertion
  Felony conviction
  Imprisonment
  Nonsupport
  Separation (1 year)
Grounds for annulment
  Bigamy
  Blood relationship
  Duress or force
  Fraud
  Insanity when married
Grounds for declaring the marriage void
  Bigamy
  Blood relationship
Residence requirement
  None
What happens with inheritance if there is no will (intestacy)?
1. If there are no surviving parents or children of deceased, surviving spouse inherits the entire estate.
2. If there are no surviving children but parents of deceased are living, the remaining spouse inherits one-half of the estate.
3. If there are surviving children of deceased, they inherit the entire estate.
Other questions
  Are holographic wills recognized? Yes
  Can support (separate maintenance) for wife and children be awarded from the time of filing for divorce until award of the final decree? Yes

Can alimony be awarded to take effect after the final decree? Yes

Can custody be awarded with the divorce (dissolution) decree? Yes

Can child support be awarded with the divorce (dissolution) decree? No

Are there dower rights? No

Can property be divided and awarded with the divorce (dissolution) decree? Yes

Is this a community property state? Yes

Can court allow wife to resume her former name? No

Is there a uniform reciprocal enforcement-of-support act? Yes

Legal Referral Service

New Orleans, LA 70130: Lawyer Referral Service, New Orleans Bar Association, Room 511, 211 Camp Street; 504-524-0495

Legal Aid

New Orleans, LA 70130: Legal Aid Bureau, Civil Division, Room 511, 211 Camp Street; 504-523-2597

Armed Forces Legal Assistance

Army: Legal Assistance Officer, Office of the Staff Judge Advocate, Fort Polk, LA 71459

Navy: Legal Assistance Officer, Headquarters, 8th Naval District, New Orleans, LA 70140; 504-366-2311, ext. 414

Air Force: Legal Assistance Office (JA), England AFB, LA 71301

Coast Guard: Legal Assistance Officer, c/o Commander 8th Coast Guard District, Hale Boggs Federal Building, 500 Camp Street, New Orleans, LA 70130; 504-589-6188

Maine

Marriage

Minimum age: male, none; female, none

Age requiring parental consent: male, under 18; female, under 18

Age not requiring parental consent: male, 18; female, 18

Blood-test requirement: yes

Waiting period: 5 days

Recognition of common-law marriage: no

Grounds for divorce

Adultery

Alcoholism

Cruelty, mental

Cruelty, physical

Desertion (3 years)

Drug addiction

Impotence at time of marriage

Mental illness (confinement for 7 years)

No-fault (irretrievable breakdown)

Nonsupport (no time limit)

Grounds for legal separation

Desertion (1 year)

Separation (1 year)

Grounds for annulment

Bigamy

Blood relationship or affinity

Duress or fraud

Final judgment sentencing either party to life imprisonment

Impotence at time of marriage

Insanity/idiocy at time of marriage

Marriage in jest

Nonage

Pregnancy

Grounds for declaring the marriage void

Bigamy

Blood relationship

Insanity/idiocy at time of marriage

Marriage out of state to evade law

Residence requirement

6 months (for divorce)

What happens with inheritance if there is no will (intestacy)?

If there are children, surviving spouse inherits one-third. If there are no children, spouse inherits two-thirds of the estate if couple were living together at time of death; otherwise, spouse inherits one-half of the estate. Where the remainder is less than $10,000 or where there is no existing kin within second degree, spouse inherits the entire estate.

Other questions

Are holographic wills recognized? No (except in the case of soldiers and sailors)

Can support (separate maintenance) for wife and children be awarded from the time of filing for divorce until award of the final decree? Yes

Can alimony be awarded to take effect after the final decree? Yes

Can custody be awarded with the divorce (dissolution) decree? Yes

Can child support be awarded with the divorce (dissolution) decree? Yes

Are there dower rights? No

Can property be divided and awarded with the divorce (dissolution) decree? Yes

Is this a community property state? No

Can court allow wife to resume her former name? Yes

Is there a uniform reciprocal enforcement-of-support act? Yes

Legal Referral Service

Augusta, ME 04330: Maine Bar Association, 154 State Street, P.O. Box 788; 207-622-7523

Legal Aid

Portland, ME: Pine Tree Legal Assistance, 178 Middle Street; 207-774-8211

Branch offices: Augusta, Bangor, Calais, Lewiston, Presque Isle, ME

Armed Forces Legal Assistance

Army: None

Navy: Legal Assistance Officer, Naval Air Station, Brunswick, ME 04011; 207-921-2331

Air Force: Legal Assistance Office (JA), Loring AFB, ME 04750; 207-999-7262, 207-999-7274

Coast Guard: None

Maryland

Marriage
Minimum age: male, 16; female, 16
Age requiring parental consent: male, under 18; female, under 18
Age not requiring parental consent: male, 18; female, 18
Blood-test requirement: no
Waiting period: 2 days
Recognition of common-law marriage: no

Grounds for divorce
Abandonment (1 year)
Adultery
Desertion
Felony conviction
Impotence at time of marriage
Insanity, postmarital (3 years)
No-fault (separated 18 months)

Grounds for legal separation
Abandonment
Cruelty, physical
Desertion

Grounds for annulment
Bigamy
Blood relationship
Insanity at time of marriage

Grounds for declaring the marriage void
Blood relationship

Residence requirement
1 year

What happens with inheritance if there is no will (intestacy)?
Spouse inherits the entire estate if there are no children; one-third if there are children.

Other questions
Are holographic wills recognized? Yes. (If executed by serviceman outside of U.S., D.C., territories, valid for 1 year only.)

Can support (separate maintenance) for wife and children be awarded from the time of filing for divorce until award of the final decree? Yes

Can alimony be awarded to take effect after the final decree? Yes

Can custody be awarded with the divorce (dissolution) decree? Yes

Can child support be awarded with the divorce (dissolution) decree? Yes

Are there dower rights? No

Can property be divided and awarded with the divorce (dissolution) decree? Yes

Is this a community property state? No

Can court allow wife to resume her former name? Yes

Is there a uniform reciprocal enforcement-of-support act? Yes

Legal Referral Service

Baltimore, MD 21202: 111 North Calvert Street, Room 629; 301-539-3112

Legal Aid

Baltimore, MD 21202: 341 North Calvert Street; 301-539-5340

Armed Forces Legal Assistance

Army: Legal Assistance Officer, Post Judge Advovocate, Building 2718, Fort George G. Meade, MD, 20755; 301-677-2576

Navy: Legal Assistance Officer, National Naval Medical Center, Bethesda, MD 20014; 301-295-0086

Air Force: Legal Assistance Officer (JA), 76 Air Base Group, Andrews AFB, MD 20331; 301-981-7331

Coast Guard: Legal Assistance Officer, U.S. Coast Guard, CCGD5 (d1 Baltimore Branch, Building 70, USCG Yard, Curtis Bay, Baltimore, MD 21226; 301-798-1600, ext. 391

Massachusetts

Marriage
Minimum age; male, 18; female, 18
Age requiring parental consent: male, under 18 cannot marry; female, under 18 cannot marry
Age not requiring parental consent: male, 18; female, 18
Blood-test requirement: yes
Waiting period: 5 days
Recognition of common-law marriage: no
Grounds for divorce
Adultery
Alcoholism
Cruelty, mental
Cruelty, physical
Desertion (2 years)
Drug addiction
Felony conviction
Impotence
Imprisonment, life
No-fault (irretrievable breakdown)
Nonsupport
Grounds for legal separation
Adultery
Alcoholism
Cruelty, mental
Cruelty, physical
Desertion
Drug addiction
Impotence
Imprisonment, life
Nonsupport
Grounds for annulment
Bigamy
Blood relationship
Fraud
Insanity at time of marriage
Nonage

Pregnancy (see page 128)
Venereal disease

Grounds for declaring the marriage void
Bigamy
Blood relationship
Nonage

Residence requirement
1 year

What happens with inheritance if there is no will (intestacy)?

If there are no children, surviving spouse inherits the entire estate. If there are children, surviving spouse inherits one-third of the estate.

Other questions
Are holographic wills recognized? No

Can support (separate maintenance) for wife and children be awarded from the time of filing for divorce until award of the final decree? Yes

Can alimony be awarded to take effect after the final decree? Yes

Can custody be awarded with the divorce (dissolution) decree? Yes

Can child support be awarded with the divorce (dissolution) decree? Yes

Are there dower rights? Yes

Can property be divided and awarded with the divorce (dissolution) decree? Yes

Is this a community property state? No

Can court allow wife to resume her former name? Yes

Is there a uniform reciprocal enforcement-of-support act? Yes

Legal Referral Service
Boston, MA 02108: Massachusetts Bar Association, 1 Center Plaza; 800-392-6164 (WATS line)

Legal Aid
Boston, MA 02109: Lawyers Committee for Civil Rights Under Law of the Boston Bar Foundation Branch, 15 State Street

Salem, MA 01970: Massachusetts Defenders Committee Office, 189 Jefferson Avenue; 617-744-4500

Armed Forces Legal Assistance
    Army: Legal Assistance Office, HQ U.S. Army Garrison, Ft. Devens, MA 01433
    Navy: Legal Assistance Officer, Naval Air Station, South Weymouth, MA 02190; 617-335-5600
    Air Force: Legal Assistance Office, (JA), L. G. Hanscom Field, Bedford, MA 01730
    Coast Guard: Legal Assistance Officer, c/o Commander 1st Coast Guard District, 150 Causeway Street, Boston, MA 02114; 617-223-5736

Michigan

Marriage
    Minimum age: male, 18; female, 16
    Age requiring parental consent: male, under 18 cannot marry; female, under 18
    Age not requiring parental consent: male, 18; female, 18
    Blood-test requirement: yes
    Waiting period: 3 days—can be waived
    Recognition of common-law marriage: yes
Grounds for divorce
    No-fault (irretrievable breakdown)
Grounds for legal separation
    No-fault (irretrievable breakdown)
Grounds for annulment
    Duress or force
    Fraud
    Idiocy
    Incapacity, physical
    Insanity
    Nonage
Grounds for declaring the marriage void
    Bigamy
    Blood relationship
    Idiocy
    Insanity
    Lack of cohabitation
    Nonage

Residence requirement
   6 months

What happens with inheritance if there is no will (intestacy)?
If there are no children, spouse inherits the entire estate. If there are children, surviving spouse inherits one-third.

Other questions
   Are holographic wills recognized? Yes (two witnesses required)

   Can support (separate maintenance) for wife and children be awarded from the time of filing for divorce until award of the final decree? Yes

   Can alimony be awarded to take effect after the final decree? Yes

   Can custody be awarded with the divorce (dissolution) decree? Yes

   Can child support be awarded with the divorce (dissolution) decree? Yes

   Are there dower rights? Yes

   Can property be divided and awarded with the divorce (dissolution) decree? Yes

   Is this a community property state? No
   Can court allow wife to resume her former name? Yes

   Is there a uniform reciprocal enforcement-of-support act? Yes

Legal Referral Service
   Lansing, MI 48933: State Bar of Michigan, 306 Townsend Street; 517-372-9030

Legal Aid
   Detroit, MI 48226: Legal Aid and Defender Association of Detroit, Law Center Building, 600 Woodward Avenue

   Lansing, MI 48933: Greater Lansing Legal Aid Bureau, P.O. Box 1071; 517-484-7773

Armed Forces Legal Assistance
   Army: Legal Assistance Office, Headquarters U.S. Army Tank-Auto Command, Warren, MI 48090

   Navy: Legal Assistance Officer, Naval Legal Service

    Office, Naval Training Center, Great Lakes, IL 60088; 312-688-3340

Air Force: Legal Assistance Office, (JA), K. I. Sawyer AFB, MI 49843; 906-346-6511, ext. 2431

Coast Guard: None

Committee on Military Law: State Bar of Michigan, 55 old Kent Building, Grand Rapids, MI 49502

Minnesota

Marriage
    Minimum age: male, 18; female, 16
    Age requiring parental consent: male, under 18 cannot marry; female, 18
    Age not requiring parental consent: male, 18; female, 18
    Blood-test requirement: no
    Waiting period: 5 days
    Recognition of common-law marriage: yes
Grounds for dissolution of marriage (divorce)
    Adultery
    Desertion
    Felony conviction
    Impotence
    Insanity, postmarital (3 years)
    No-fault (irretrievable breakdown: any of other grounds listed can be used as supporting evidence)
Grounds for legal separation
    Insanity, postmarital
    Separation (continuous for 5 years)
Grounds for annulment
    Bigamy
    Blood relationship
    Duress or force
    Fraud
    Insanity at time of marriage
    Nonage

Grounds for declaring the marriage void
  Bigamy
  Blood relationship
  Nonage
Residence requirement
  1 year
What happens with inheritance if there is no will (intestacy)?
If there are no children, spouse inherits the entire estate. If there is one child surviving spouse inherits one-half. If there is more than one child surving, spouse inherits one-third.
Other questions
  Are holographic wills recognized? No
  Can support (separate maintenance) for wife and children be awarded from the time of filing for divorce until award of the final decree? Yes
  Can alimony be awarded to take effect after the final decree? Yes
  Can custody be awarded with the divorce (dissolution) decree? Yes
  Can child support be awarded with the divorce (dissolution) decree? Yes
  Are there dower rights? No
  Can property be divided and awarded with the divorce (dissolution) decree? Yes
  Is this a community property state? No
  Can court allow wife to resume her former name? Yes
  Is there a uniform reciprocal enforcement-of-support act? Yes
Legal Referral Service
  Minneapolis, MN 55402: Minnesota State Bar Association, 510 Syndicate Building; 612-338-1846
Legal Aid
  Minneapolis, MN 55415: Legal Aid Society of Minneapolis, 501 Park Avenue; 612-332-1441
Armed Forces Legal Assistance
  Army: 128th JAG Detachment (Army Reserve), Building, 101A, Fort Snelling, MN 55111; 612-726-1551, ext. 668

Navy: Legal Assistance Officer, Naval Legal Service Office, Naval Training Center, Great Lakes, IL 60088; 312-688-3340

Air Force: Legal Assistance Officer, (JA), Duluth International Airport, Duluth, MN 55814

Coast Guard: None

Mississippi

Marriage
   Minimum age: male, 17; female, 15
   Age requiring parental consent: male, under 21; female, under 21
   Age not requiring parental consent: male, 21; female, 21
   Blood test requirement: yes
   Waiting period: 3 days
   Recognition of common-law marriage: only if contracted before April 5, 1956

Grounds for divorce
   Adultery
   Alcoholism
   Bigamy
   Blood relationship
   Cruelty, mental (inhuman treatment), habitual
   Cruelty, physical (inhuman treatment), habitual
   Desertion (1 year)
   Drug addiction
   Felony conviction (interned in penitentiary)
   Impotence
   Imprisonment, life
   Insanity at time of marriage
   Insanity, postmarital (3 years)
   No-fault (irretrievable breakdown)
   Pregnancy (see page 128)

Grounds for legal separation
   Separate maintenance without divorce at court's discretion

Grounds for annulment
   Bigamy

Blood relationship
Duress or force
Fraud
Impotence
Insanity at time of marriage
Malformation preventing intercourse
Nonage
Pregnancy (see page 128)

Grounds for declaring the marriage void
Bigamy
Blood relationship

Residence requirement
6 months

What happens with inheritance if there is no will (intestacy)?
Surviving spouse inherits entire estate if there are no children. If there are children, spouse shares inheritance equally with them.

Other questions
Are holographic wills recognized? Yes
Can support (separate maintenance) for wife and children be awarded from the time of filing for divorce until award of the final decree? Yes
Can alimony be awarded to take effect after the final decree? Yes
Can custody be awarded with the divorce (dissolution) decree? Yes
Can child support be awarded with the divorce (dissolution) decree? Yes
Are there dower rights? No
Can property be divided and awarded with the divorce (dissolution) decree? Yes
Is this a community property state? No
Can court allow wife to resume her former name? Yes
Is there a uniform reciprocal enforcement-of-support act? Yes

Legal Referral Service
Jackson, MS 39205: Hinds County Bar Association; Robert E. Lee State Building, 601-948-4651

Legal Aid
Jackson, MS 39204: Legal Aid of Jackson, Pub-

lic Welfare Building, P.O. Box 8777; 601-373-
1120

Armed Forces Legal Assistance
Army: None
Navy: Legal Assistance Officer, Naval Air Station,
Meridian, MS 39301; 601-679-8211, ext. 391
Air Force: Legal Assistance Office (JA), Keesler
AFB, MS 39534
Coast Guard: None
Military Law and Legal Assistance for Service Men
Committee: Mississippi State Bar, P.O. Box
724, Jackson, MS 39205

Missouri

Marriage
Minimum age: male, 15; female, 15
Age requiring parental consent: male, under 18; fe-
male, under 18
Age not requiring parental consent: male, 18; fe-
male, 18
Blood-test requirement: yes
Waiting period: 3 days
Recognition of common-law marriage: no
Grounds for dissolution of marriage (divorce)
Adultery
Alcoholism
Conviction of felony
Cruelty, mental (treatment endangering life)
Cruelty, physical (treatment endangering life)
Desertion (1 year)
Impotence
No-fault (irretrievable breakdown)
Personal indignities
Pregnancy (see page 128)
Vagrancy of husband
Grounds for legal separation
See grounds for dissolution of marriage.
Grounds for declaring the marriage void
Bigamy

Blood relationship
Insanity at time of marriage
Residence requirement
90 days
What happens with inheritance if there is no will (intestacy)?
If there are no children, surviving spouse inherits the entire estate. If there are children, spouse inherits one-half.
Other questions
Are holographic wills recognized? No
Can support (separate maintenance) for wife and children be awarded from the time of filing for divorce until award of the final decree? Yes
Can alimony be awarded to take effect after the final decree? Yes
Can custody be awarded with the divorce (dissolution) decree? Yes
Can child support be awarded with the divorce (dissolution) decree? Yes
Are there dower rights? No
Can property be divided and awarded with the divorce (dissolution) decree? Yes
Is this a community property state? No
Can court allow wife to resume her former name? No
Is there a uniform reciprocal enforcement-of-support act? Yes
Legal Referral Service
St. Louis, MO 63105: Lawyer's Reference Service Bar Association of Metropolitan St. Louis and St. Louis County Bar, Civil Courts Building, 7900 Forsyth Boulevard; 314-421-6154
Legal Aid
St. Louis, MO 63110: Legal Aid Society of the City and County of St. Louis, Room 409, 4030 Chouteau Avenue; 314-652-9581
Armed Forces Legal Assistance
Army: Legal Assistance Office, U.S. Army Administration Center, 9700 Page Boulevard, St. Louis, MO 63132

Navy: Legal Assistance Officer, Naval Legal Service
Office, Naval Training Center, Great Lakes, IL
60088; 312-688-3340

Air Force: Legal Assistance Office (JA), Whiteman
AFB, MO 65301; 816-563-5511, exts. 3422,
3243

Coast Guard: Legal Assistance Officer, c/o Commander 2d Coast Guard District, Federal Building, 1520 Market Street, St. Louis, MO 63103;
314-425-4626

Montana

Marriage
Minimum age: male, 16; female, 16
Age requiring parental consent: male, under 18; fe-
male, under 18
Age not requiring parental consent: male, 18; fe-
male, 18
Blood-test requirement: yes
Waiting period: 3 days
Recognition of common-law marriage: yes
Grounds for dissolution of marriage (divorce)
No-fault (irretrievable breakdown)
Grounds for legal separation
No-fault (irretrievable breakdown)
Grounds for declaration of invalidity
Bigamy (marriage is prohibited)
Blood relationship
Force or duress
Fraud
Lack of capacity to consent to marriage at time it
was entered into
Lack of physical capacity to consummate marriage
by sexual intercourse
Nonage
Residence requirement
90 days
What happens with inheritance if there is no will
(intestacy)?
1. If there are no surviving children of deceased or if

there are surviving children all of whom are of the surviving spouse, surviving spouse inherits the entire estate.

2. Spouse inherits one-half of the estate if there are children one or more of whom are not issue of the surviving spouse, if there are offspring of such child or children. Spouse inherits one-third of the estate if there is more than one such child, or one such child and the issue of one or more deceased children.

Other questions

Are holographic wills recognized? Yes

Can support (separate maintenance) for wife and children be awarded from the time of filing for divorce until award of the final decree? Yes

Can maintenance be awarded to take effect after the final decree? Yes

Can custody be awarded with the divorce (dissolution) decree? Yes

Can child support be awarded with the divorce (dissolution) decree? Yes

Are there dower rights? No

Can property be divided and awarded with the divorce (dissolution) decree? Yes

Is this a community property state? No

Can court allow wife to resume her former name? Yes

Is there a uniform reciprocal enforcement-of-support act? Yes

Legal Referral Service

Helena, MT 59601: State Bar of Montana, 2030 11th Avenue; 406-442-7613

Legal Aid

Billings, MT 59711: Yellowstone County Legal Services, Montana Legal Services Association Branch, 2822 3d Avenue, N; 406-248-7113

Helena, MT 59601: Montana Legal Services Association, 601 Power Block; 406-442-9830

And other branch offices

Armed Forces Legal Assistance

Army: None

Navy: Legal Assistance Officer, Naval Legal Service Office, Seattle, WA 98115; 206-527-3835

Air Force: Legal Assistance Office, (JA), Malstrom, AFB, MT 59402; 406-731-3486, 406-731-3486

Coast Guard: None

Nebraska

Marriage

Minimum age: male, 18; female, 16

Age requiring parental consent: male, under 19; female, under 19

Age not requiring parental consent: male, 19; female, 19

Blood-test requirement: yes

Waiting period: 2 days

Recognition of common-law marriage: no

Grounds for dissolution of marriage (divorce)

No-fault (irretrievable breakdown)

Grounds for legal separation

No-fault (irretrievable breakdown)

Grounds for annulment

Bigamy

Blood relationship

Force or duress

Fraud

Impotence at time of marriage

Insanity at time of marriage

Nonage

Grounds for declaring the marriage void

Bigamy

Blood relationship

Insanity at time of marriage

Residence requirement

1 year

What happens with inheritance if there is no will (intestacy)?

1. If there are no surviving parents or children of deceased, surviving spouse inherits the entire estate.

2. If there are no surviving children but parents of

deceased are living, surviving spouse inherits $35,-000 and one-half of the balance of the estate.

3. If there are children of surviving spouse, spouse inherits the first $35,000 and one-half of the balance of the estate.

4. If there are children one or more of whom are not issue of surviving spouse, spouse inherits one-half of the estate.

Other questions

Are holographic wills recognized? Yes

Can support (separate maintenance) for wife and children be awarded from the time of filing for divorce until award of the final decree? Ycs

Can alimony be awarded to take effect after the final decree? Yes

Can custody be awarded with the divorce (dissolution) decree? Yes

Can child support be awarded with the divorce (dissolution) decree? Yes

Are there dower rights? No

Can property be divided and awarded with the divorce (dissolution) decree? Yes

Is this a community property state? No

Can court allow wife to resume her former name? Not ordinarily. But the law relating to driver's licenses (section 60–415) suggests it is possible.

Is there a uniform reciprocal enforcement-of-support act? Yes

Legal Referral Service

Lincoln, NE 68508: Lincoln Bar Association, 800 Anderson Building; 402-435-2161

Omaha, NE 68178: Omaha Bar Association, 2500 California Street; 402-341-4104

Legal Aid

Lincoln, NE 68508: 800 Anderson Building

Omaha, NE 68102: Legal Aid Society of Omaha and Council Bluffs, 1613 Farnam Street

Armed Forces Legal Assistance

Army: Legal Assistance Officer, 121st JAG Detachment (Army Reserve), 21st and Woolworth Streets, Omaha, NE 68108

Navy: Legal Assistance Officer, Naval Legal Service Office, Naval Training Center, Great Lakes, IL 60088; 312-688-3340

Air Force: Legal Assistance Office, (JA), 3902 Air Base Wing, Offutt AFB, NE 68113; 402-294-3732

Coast Guard: None

Nevada

Marriage
    Minimum age: male, 16; female, 16
    Age requiring parental consent: male, under 18; female, under 18
    Age not requiring parental consent: male, 18; female, 18
    Blood-test requirement: no
    Waiting period: none
    Recognition of common-law marriage: no
Grounds for divorce
    Insanity, postmarital (2 years)
    No-fault (incompatibility)
    Separation (1 year)
Grounds for separate maintenance (legal separation)
    Any cause of action for divorce
    Desertion (90 days)
Grounds for annulment
    Bigamy
    Blood relationship
    Fraud
    Insanity at time of marriage
    Nonage
    Other grounds (grounds that the court finds for declaring the marital contract void)
Grounds for declaring the marriage void
    Bigamy
    Blood relationship
Residence requirement
    6 weeks

What happens with inheritance if there is no will (intestacy)?

If there are no children, spouse inherits the entire estate. If there is one child surviving, spouse inherits one-half. If there is more than one child surviving, spouse inherits one-third.

Other questions

Are holographic wills recognized? Yes

Can support (separate maintenance) for wife and children be awarded from the time of filing for divorce until award of the final decree? Yes

Can alimony be awarded to take effect after the final decree? Yes

Can custody be awarded with the divorce (dissolution) decree? Yes

Can child support be awarded with the divorce (dissolution) decree? Yes

Are there dower rights? No

Can property be divided and awarded with the divorce (dissolution) decree? Yes

Is this a community property state? Yes

Can court allow wife to resume her former name? Yes

Is there a uniform reciprocal enforcement-of-support act? Yes

Legal Referral Service

Las Vegas, NV 89106: Clark County Bar Association, 301 South Highland Drive; 702-395-5240

Legal Aid

Las Vegas, NV 89106: Clark County Legal Service Program, 900 West Bonanza Road; 702-648-6970

Armed Forces Legal Assistance

Army: None

Navy: Legal Assistance Officer, Naval Legal Service Office, Naval Station Treasure Island, San Francisco, CA 94130; 415-765-5287

Air Force: Legal Assistance Office (JA), Nellis AFB NV 89110

Coast Guard: None

New Hampshire

Marriage
    Minimum age: male, 14; female, 13
    Age requiring parental consent: male, under 18; female, under 18
    Age not requiring parental consent: male, 18; female, 18
    Blood-test requirement: yes
    Waiting period: 5 days
    Recognition of common-law marriage: no
Grounds for divorce
    Abandonment (1 year)
    Adultery
    Alcoholism (2 years)
    Cruelty, mental (extreme)
    Cruelty, physical (extreme)
    Desertion (2 years)
    Felony conviction (at time of suit, with commitment of 1 year or more)
    Impotence
    Imprisonment (1 year or more)
    Joining a religious sect and as a consequence not cohabitating for 6 months
    Malformation preventing intercourse
    No-fault (irreconcilable differences)
    Nonsupport (2 years)
    Refusal to cohabit (6 months)
    Separation (1 year)
Grounds for legal separation
    Any grounds for divorce
    Desertion (2 years)
Grounds for annulment
    Bigamy
    Blood relationship
    Neglect (husband or wife absent and unheard of for 2 years; wife absent for 10 years, beyond state, without his consent; husband or wife joining a

religious sect that holds marriage unlawful and refusing to cohabit for 6 months)

Grounds for declaring the marriage void
   Bigamy
   Blood relationship

Residence requirement
   1 year

What happens with inheritance if there is no will (intestacy)?

If there are children, surviving spouse inherits one-third of the estate. If there are no children, surviving spouse receives $10,000 and $2,000 for each full year of marriage until death of spouse and one-half of the remaining estate. Where inventory of real estate does not exceed $10,000, the surviving spouse inherits the entire remaining estate.

Other questions
   Are holographic wills recognized? No
   Can support (separate maintenance) for wife and children be awarded from the time of filing for divorce until award of the final decree? Yes
   Can alimony be awarded to take effect after the final decree? Yes
   Can custody be awarded with the divorce (dissolution) decree? Yes
   Can child support be awarded with the divorce (dissolution) decree? Yes
   Are there dower rights? No
   Can property be divided and awarded with the divorce (dissolution) decree? Yes
   Is this a community property state? No
   Can court allow wife to resume her former name? Yes
   Is there a uniform reciprocal enforcement-of-support act? Yes

Legal Referral Service
   Manchester, NH 03101: New Hampshire Bar Association, 77 Market Street; 603-669-3333

Legal Aid
   Concord, NH 03301: New Hampshire Legal Assistance Branch, 136 North Main; 603-224-3333

Armed Forces Legal Assistance
  Army: None
  Navy: Legal Assistance Officer, Naval Shipyard, Portsmouth, NH 03801; 207-439-1000, ext. 703
  Air Force: Legal Assistance Office (JA), Pease AFB, NH 03801; 603-436-0100, exts. 2126, 2125
  Coast Guard: None

New Jersey

Marriage
  Minimum age: male, 18; female, 16
  Age requiring parental consent: male, under 18 cannot marry; female, under 18
  Age not requiring parental consent: male, 18; female, 18
  Blood-test requirement: yes
  Waiting period: 3 days
  Recognition of common-law marriage: no
Grounds for divorce
  Adultery
  Alcoholism (1 year)
  Confinement in mental institution
  Cruelty (extreme)
  Desertion (1 year)
  Deviant sexual behavior
  Drug addiction
  Drunkenness (12 months)
  Imprisonment (12 or more months)
  Insanity, postmarital (2 years)
  No-fault (separation for 18 months)
Grounds for legal separation
  See grounds for divorce.
Grounds for annulment
  Bigamy
  Blood relationship
  Force or duress
  Fraud
  Impotence (if undisclosed at time of marriage)

Insanity at time of marriage

Nonage

Grounds for declaring the marriage void

See grounds for annulment.

Residence requirement

1 year

What happens with inheritance if there is no will (intestacy)?

If there are no children, the spouse inherits the entire estate.

Other questions

Are holographic wills recognized? Yes

Can support (separate maintenance) for wife and children be awarded from the time of filing for divorce until award of the final decree? Yes

Can alimony be awarded to take effect after the final decree? Yes

Can custody be awarded with the divorce (dissolution) decree? Yes

Can child support be awarded with the divorce (dissolution) decree? Yes

Are there dower rights? Yes

Can property be divided and awarded with the divorce (dissolution) decree? Yes

Is this a community property state? No

Can court allow wife to resume her former name? Yes

Is there a uniform reciprocal enforcement-of-support act? Yes

Legal Referral Service

Newark, NJ 07102: Essex County Bar Association, 92 Washington Street, 201-622-6207

Trenton, NJ 08608: Mercer County Bar Association, 440 East State Street; 609-695-6249, 609-988-8880

Legal Aid

Newark, NJ 07050: Essex County Legal Service Corporation, 463 Central Avenue

Trenton, NJ 08608: Legal Aid Society of Mercer County, 440 East State Street

Armed Forces Legal Assistance
  Army: Legal Assistance Office, Military Olean Terminal, Bayonne, NJ 07002
  Navy: Legal Assistance Officer, Naval Air Station Lakehurst, NJ 08733; 201-323-2571
  Air Force: Legal Assistance Office (JA), 438 Air Base Group, McGuire AFB, NJ 08641
  Coast Guard: Base Legal Officer, U.S. Coast Guard Training Center, Cape May, NJ 08204; 609-884-8451, ext. 210

New Mexico

Marriage
  Minimum age: male, 16; female, 16
  Age requiring parental consent: male, under 18; female, under 18
  Age not requiring parental consent: male, 18; female, 18
  Blood-test requirement: yes
  Waiting period: none
  Recognition of common-law marriage: no
Grounds for dissolution of marriage
  Abandonment
  Adultery
  Cruelty
  No-fault (incompatibility)
Grounds for divorce
  Abandonment
  Adultery
  Cruelty, mental
  Cruelty, physical
  No-fault (incompatibility)
Grounds for legal separation
  Separation (voluntarily living apart)
Grounds for annulment
  Blood relationship
  Nonage
Grounds for declaring the marriage void
  Bigamy
  Blood relationship

Residence requirement
6 months

What happens with inheritance if there is no will (intestacy)?
1. If there are no surviving children of deceased, surviving spouse inherits the entire estate.
2. If there are children of surviving spouse, spouse inherits one-fourth of the estate.
3. Because this is a community property state, the above provisions apply only to the separate properties of deceased.

Other questions
Are holographic wills recognized? No
Can support (separate maintenance) for wife and children be awarded from the time of filing for divorce until award of the final decree? Yes
Can alimony be awarded to take effect after the final decree? Yes
Can custody be awarded with the divorce (dissolution decree? Yes
Can child support be awarded with the divorce (dissolution) decree? Yes
Are there dower rights? No
Can property be divided and awarded with the divorce (dissolution) decree? Yes
Is this a community property state? Yes
Can court allow wife to resume her former name? Yes
Is there a uniform reciprocal enforcement-of-support act? Yes

Legal Referral Service
Albuquerque, NM 87102: Albuquerque Bar Association, 911 Sandia Savings Building; 505-243-2615
Santa Fe, NM 87501: 1st Judicial District Bar Association, 105 East Marcy Street, Room 134; 505-982- 4737

Legal Aid
Albuquerque, NM 87101: 1015 Tijeras Avenue, NW; 505-242-3442
Santa Fe, NM 87501: 322 Montezuma Street; 505-982-9886

Armed Forces Legal Assistance
   Army: Office of the Staff Judge Advocate, White
      Sands Missile Range, NM 88002
   Navy: Legal Assistance Officer, Naval Legal Service
      Office, Naval Air Station, Corpus Christi, NM
      78419; 512-939-3765
   Air Force: Legal Assistance Office (JA), Kirtland
      AFB, NM 87115
   Coast Guard: None

New York

Marriage
   Minimum age: male, 16; female, 14
   Age requiring parental consent: male, under 18: fe-
      male under 18
   Age not requiring parental consent: male, 18; female,
      18
   Blood-test requirement: yes
   Waiting period: 10 days
   Recognition of common-law marriage: no (unless
      created in another state)
Grounds for dissolution of marriage
   Spouse absent for 5 years with whereabouts unknown
      and assumed dead after search
Grounds for divorce
   Adultery
   Cruelty, mental
   Cruelty, physical
   Felony conviction (commitment to prison for 3
      years)
   No-fault (separated for 1 year)
   Separation (living apart for 1 year after decree of
      separation or after properly filed and executed sep-
      aration agreement)
Grounds for legal separation
   Abandonment
   Adultery
   Cruelty, mental
   Cruelty, physical

Felony conviction (commitment to prison for 3 years)

Nonsupport

Grounds for annulment

Bigamy (marriage is void)

Blood relationship (marriage is void)

Force or duress

Fraud

Impotence at time of marriage

Life imprisonment (ground for declaring marriage void)

Mental incompetence at marriage

Insanity, postmarital (5 years: obligation to support insane spouse is not removed with decree)

Malformation preventing intercourse

Nonage

Sterility unknown at marriage

Residence requirement

Time varies from none, if cause of action occurred in the state and both parties are residents, to 2 years, if neither cause of action nor marriage occurred in state and only one partner is resident.

What happens with inheritance if there is no will (intestacy)?

If there is more than one child, surviving spouse inherits personal property up to $2,000 and one-third of the remaining estate. If there is one child, spouse inherits $2,000 and one-half of the remaining estate. If deceased left no children, but relatives specified by New York law, spouse inherits $25,000 and one-half of the remaining estate. If there are neither children nor aforementioned relatives, spouse inherits the entire estate.

Other questions

Are holographic wills recognized? Only valid for (1) active military personnel and persons serving with or accompanying a military force engaged in war or other armed conflict; (2) marines at sea

Can support (separate maintenance) for wife and

children be awarded from the time of filing for divorce until award of the final decree? Yes

Can alimony be awarded to take effect after the final decree? Yes

Can custody be awarded with the divorce (dissolution) decree? Yes

Can child support be awarded with the divorce (dissolution) decree? Yes

Are there dower rights? No (unless married before 1930)

Can property be divided and awarded with the divorce (dissolution) decree? No

Is this a community property state? No

Can court allow wife to resume her former name? No

Is there a uniform reciprocal enforcement-of-support act? Yes

Legal Referral Service

Albany, NY 11207: Albany County Bar Association, Room 315, County Court House; 518-445-7691

New York, NY 10036: Association of the Bar of New York and New York Lawyers' Association, 42 West 44th Street; 212-687-7383

Legal Aid

Albany, NY 12207: 79 North Pearl Street; 518-462-6765

New York, NY 10013: Community Action for Legal Services, 335 Broadway; 212-966-6600

Armed Forces Legal Assistance

Army: Legal Assistance Office, U.S. Military Academy, West Point, NY 10996

Navy: Legal Assistance Officer, 3d Naval District, Headquarters, NSSNF Building, Brooklyn, NY 11251; 212-834-2316, ext. 320

Air Force: Legal Assistance Office (JA), Griffiss AFB, NY 13441

Coast Guard: Legal Assistance Office, c/o Commander 3d Coast Guard District, Governors Island, NY 10004; 212-264-8740

North Carolina

Marriage
Minimum age: male, 16, female, 16
Age requiring parental consent: male, under 18;
female, under 18
Age not requiring parental consent: male, 18; fe-
male, 18
Blood-test requirement: yes
Waiting period: yes
Recognition of common-law marriage: no
Grounds for divorce
Adultery
Crimes against nature
Impotence
Imprisonment resulting in involuntary separation be-
cause of a criminal act
Insanity, postmarital (5 years)
No-fault (separation for 1 year)
Pregnancy (see page 128)
Grounds for legal separation
Abandonment
Alcoholism
Cruelty, mental
Cruelty, physical
Drug addiction
Maliciously turning the other spouse out of doors
Personal indignities
Grounds for annulment
Bigamy
Blood relationship
Insanity at time of marriage
Nonage
Grounds for declaring the marriage void
Bigamy
Blood relationship
Impotence at time of marriage
Insanity at time of marriage

Residence requirement
　6 months

What happens with inheritance if there is no will (intestacy)?

　If there is one child, surviving spouse inherits one-half of the estate. If there is more than one child, surviving spouse inherits one-third of the estate. If there is no child, surviving spouse inherits entire estate.

Other questions

　Are holographic wills recognized? Yes

　Can support (separate maintenance) for wife and children be awarded from the time of filing for divorce until award of the final decree? Yes

　Can alimony be awarded to take effect after the final decree? Yes

　Can custody be awarded with the divorce (dissolution) decree? Yes

　Can child support be awarded with the divorce (dissolution) decree? Yes

　Are there dower rights? No

　Can property be divided and awarded with the divorce (dissolution) decree? Yes

　Is this a community property state? No

　Can court allow wife to resume her former name? Yes

　Is there a uniform reciprocal enforcement-of-support act? Yes

Legal Referral Service

　Raleigh, NC 27605: North Carolina Bar Association, 1025 Wade Avenue; 919-838-0561, 800-662-7660

Legal Aid

　Durham, NC 27701: 353 West Main Street, P.O. Box 2101

　Winston-Salem, NC 27101: Legal Aid Society of Forsyth County, 202 W. 3d Street; 919-723-4301

Armed Forces Legal Assistance

　Army: Legal Assistance Office, XVIII ABN and Fort Bragg, Office of the Staff Judge Advocate, Fort Bragg, NC 28307

　Navy: Legal Assistance Officer, Naval Legal Service

Office, Naval Base, Charleston, SC 29408: 803-
743-4740
Air Force: Legal Assistance Office (JA), Pope
AFB, NC 28308
Coast Guard: None
Military Law Committee: North Carolina Bar As-
sociation, Carolina Power & Light Company
Building, Room 312, Wilmington, NC 28401

North Dakota

Marriage
Minimum age: male, 16; female, 16
Age requiring parental consent: male, under 18; fe-
male, under 18
Age not requiring parental consent: male, 18; fe-
male, 18
Blood-test requirement: yes
Waiting period: none
Recognition of common-law marriage: no
Grounds for divorce
Abandonment (1 year)
Adultery
Alcoholism (1 year)
Cruelty, mental
Cruelty, physical
Desertion (1 year)
Drug addiction (1 year)
Felony conviction
Insanity, postmarital (5 years)
Neglect, willful (1 year)
No-fault (irreconcilable differences)
Nonsupport
Refusal to cohabit
Separation (1 year)
Grounds for legal separation
Abandonment (1 year)
Adultery
Alcoholism (1 year)
Cruelty, mental

Cruelty, physical
Desertion (1 year)
Drug addiction
Felony conviction
Insanity, postmarital (5 years)
Nonsupport
Refusal to cohabit
Separation (1 year)

Grounds for annulment
Bigamy
Blood relationship
Force or duress
Fraud
Impotence (if it continues and appears to be incurable)
Insanity at time of marriage
Malformation preventing intercourse (if it continues and appears to be incurable)
Nonage

Grounds for declaring the marriage void
Bigamy
Blood relationship

Residence requirement
1 year

What happens with inheritance if there is no will (intestacy)?

1. If there are no surviving children or parents of decedent, the entire estate goes to surviving spouse.
2. If there are no surviving children but decedent has a parent or parents still living, surviving spouse is given the first $50,000 and one-half of the balance of the intestate estate.
3. If there are surviving children of both decedent and surviving spouse, spouse receives the first $50,000 and one-half of the balance of the intestate estate.
4. If the decedent left surviving children one or more of whom are not children of the surviving spouse, spouse receives one-half of the intestate estate.
5. That part of the intestate estate not passing to surviving spouse, or all the intestate estate if there is no surviving spouse, goes to children of decedent.

6. If there are no surviving children, the entire intestate estate goes to decedent's parents equally.
7. If none of the above survive, the entire intestate estate goes to the brothers and sisters of the decedent.

Other questions

Are holographic wills recognized? Yes

Can support (separate maintenance) for wife and children be awarded from the time of filing for divorce until award of the final decree? Yes

Can alimony be awarded to take effect after the final decree? Yes

Can custody be awarded with the divorce (dissolution) decree? Yes

Can child support be awarded with the divorce (dissolution) decree? Yes

Are there dower rights? No

Can property be divided and awarded with the divorce (dissolution) decree? Yes

Is this a community property state? No

Can court allow wife to resume her former name? Yes

Is there a uniform reciprocal enforcement-of-support act? Yes

Legal Referral Service

Fargo, ND 58102: Cass County Bar Association, Legal Aid Society, 15 South 21st Street; 701-232-4495

Legal Aid

Bismarck, ND 58501: LAND, 420 North 4th Street; 701-258-4270

Devils Lake, ND 58301: LAND, 1219 College Drive; 701-662-8123

Fargo, ND 58102: Legal Aid Society of North Dakota (LAND), 15 South 21st Street; 701-232-4495

Minot, ND 58701: LAND, P.O. Box 117; 701-852-3870

Note: The school of law at the University of North Dakota in Grand Forks also operates a Legal Aid Society, independent of LAND.

Armed Forces Legal Assistance
Army: None
Navy: Legal Assistance Officer, Naval Legal Service
Office, Naval Training Center, Great Lakes, IL
60088; 312-688-3340
Air Force: Legal Assistance Office (JA), Pope
AFB, ND 28308
Coast Guard: None

Ohio

Marriage
Minimum age: male, 18; female, 16
Age requiring parental consent: male, under 18
cannot marry; female, under 18
Age not requiring parental consent: male, 18; fe-
male, 18
Blood-test requirement: yes
Waiting period: 5 days
Recognition of common-law marriage: yes
Grounds for divorce
Adultery
Alcoholism
Bigamy
Cruelty, physical
Desertion (1 year)
Fraud
Felony conviction (if imprisoned at time of suit)
Impotence
No-fault (separation for 2 years)
Nonsupport (gross neglect of duty)
Grounds for legal separation
Abandonment
Adultery
Alcoholism
Grounds for annulment
Bigamy
Force or duress
Fraud
Insanity at time of marriage

Insanity, postmarital .
Marriage never consummated
Nonage
Grounds for declaring the marriage void
Blood relationship
Residence requirement
1 year
What happens with inheritance if there is no will (intestacy)?
If there are no children, spouse inherits the entire estate. If there is one child surviving, spouse inherits the first $30,000 and one-half of the remaining estate. If there is more than one child surviving, spouse inherits the first $30,000 and one-third of the remaining estate.
Other questions
Are holographic wills recognized? No
Can support (separate maintenance) for wife and children be awarded from the time of filing for divorce until award of the final decree? Yes
Can alimony be awarded to take effect after the final decree? Yes
Can custody be awarded with the divorce (dissolution) decree? Yes
Can child support be awarded with the divorce (dissolution) decree? Yes
Are there dower rights? Yes
Can property be divided and awarded with the divorce (dissolution) decree? Yes
Is this a community property state? No
Can court allow the wife to resume her former name? Yes
Is there a uniform reciprocal enforcement-of-support act? Yes
Legal Referral Service
Columbus, OH 43201: Ohio State Bar Association, 33 West 11th Avenue; 614-421-2121
Legal Aid
Cleveland, OH 44114: Legal Aid Society of Cleveland, 2108 Payne Avenue; 216-861-6264
Columbus, OH 43210: Legal Clinic, Ohio State

University, 1659 North High Street; 614-293-
6821

Armed Forces Legal Assistance

Army: Legal Assistance Officer, 9th JAG Detachment (Army Reserve), 5301 Hauserman Road,
Parma, OH 44130

Navy: Legal Assistance Officer, Naval Legal Service
Office, Naval Base, Philadelphia, PA 19112; 215-
755-4526

Air Force: 2750 Air Base (JA), Wright-Patterson
AFB, OH 45433

Coast Guard: Legal Assistance Office, c/o Commander 9th Coast Guard District, 1240 East
9th Street, Cleveland, OH 44199; 216-522-
3903

Oklahoma

Marriage

Minimum age: male, 16; female, 16

Age requiring parental consent: male, under 18; female, under 18

Age not requiring parental consent: male, 18; female, 18

Blood-test requirement: yes

Waiting period: none

Recognition of common-law marriage: yes

Grounds for divorce

Abandonment (1 year)

Adultery

Alcoholism

Cruelty, mental

Cruelty, physical

Felony conviction (if imprisoned at time of suit)

Impotence

Insanity, postmarital

Neglect, willful

No-fault (incompatibility)

Other grounds (such as attempt to obtain divorce
outside of state)

Pregnancy (see page 128)

Grounds for legal separation

Abandonment (1 year)

Adultery

Alcoholism

Cruelty, mental

Cruelty, physical

Felony conviction (if imprisoned at time of suit)

Fraud

Impotence

Insanity, postmarital (5 years)

Neglect, willful

No-fault (incompatibility)

Other grounds (such as attempt to obtain divorce outside of state)

Pregnancy (see page 128)

Grounds for annulment

Insanity at time of marriage

Nonage

Grounds for declaring the marriage void

Bigamy

Blood relationship

Residence requirement

6 months

What happens with inheritance if there is no will (intestacy)?

If there are no children, surviving spouse inherits the entire estate. If there is one child, spouse inherits one-half of the estate. If there is more than one child, spouse inherits one-third of the estate.

Other questions

Are holographic wills recognized? Yes

Can support (separate maintenance) for wife and children be awarded from the time of filing for divorce until award of the final decree? Yes

Can alimony be awarded to take effect after the final decree? No

Can custody be awarded with the divorce (dissolution) decree? Yes

Can child support be awarded with the divorce (dissolution) decree? Yes

Are there dower rights? No

Can property be divided and awarded with the divorce (dissolution) decree? Yes

Is this a community property state? No

Can court allow the wife to resume her former name? Yes

Is there a uniform reciprocal enforcement-of-support act? Yes

Legal Referral Service

Oklahoma City, OK 73102: Oklahoma County Bar Association, 311 North Harvey Avenue, Suite 102; 405-235-6022

Legal Aid

Oklahoma City, OK 73102: 601 Mercantile Building; 405-272-9461

Armed Forces Legal Assistance

Army: Legal Assistance Office Headquarters U.S. Army Field Artillery Center and Fort Sill, Fort Sill, OK 73505

Navy: Legal Assistance Officer, Headquarters 8th Naval District, New Orleans, LA 70140; 504-366-2311, ext. 414

Air Force: Legal Assistance Office (JA), Vance AFB, OK 73701

Coast Guard: None

Legal Assistance for Service Men Committee: Oklahoma Bar Association, 314 American Building, Box 1631, Ada, OK 74820

Oregon

Marriage

Minimum age: male, 17; female, 17

Age requiring parental consent: male, under 18; female, under 18

Age not requiring parental consent: male, 18; female, 18

Blood-test requirement: yes

Waiting period: 7 days

Recognition of common-law marriage: no

Grounds for dissolution of marriage (divorce)
Force
Fraud
Incapability of understanding marriage contract
No-fault (irreconcilable differences)
Nonage

Grounds for legal separation
No-fault (irreconcilable differences)
Separation (1 year after filing a legal separation agreement)

Grounds for annulment
See grounds for dissolution of marriage.

Residence requirement
Where the parties were married in Oregon, it is sufficient that either party is a resident of or domiciled in the state at the time the suit is begun. However, where the parties were married in a state other than Oregon, at least one party must be a resident of or be domiciled in Oregon at the time the suit is begun and continuously for a period of 6 months before that time.

What happens with inheritance if there is no will (intestacy)?
If there are no children, surviving spouse inherits the entire estate. If there are children, surviving spouse inherits one-half of the estate.

Other questions
Are holographic wills recognized? No
Can support (separate maintenance) for wife and children be awarded from the time of filing for divorce until award of the final decree? There are provisions for children, but not for the wife.
Can alimony be awarded to take effect after the final decree? No
Can custody be awarded with the divorce (dissolution) decree? Yes
Can child support be awarded with the divorce (dissolution) decree? Yes
Are there dower rights? No
Can property be divided and awarded with the divorce (dissolution) decree? Yes

Is this a community property state? No

Can court allow wife to resume her former name? Yes

Is there a uniform reciprocal enforcement-of-support act? Yes

Legal Referral Service

Portland, OR 97205: Oregon State Bar Association, 1776 Southwest Madison Street; 503-229-5788

Legal Aid

Eugene, OR 97401: Lane County Legal Aid Service, 1309 Willamette Street

Multnomah, OR 97204: Multnomah County Bar Association, Room 402, 732 Southwest 3d Avenue; 503-224-4086

Armed Forces Legal Assistance

Army: None

Navy: Legal Assistance Officer, Naval Legal Service Station, Naval Base, Charleston, OR 97420; 503-743-4740

Air Force: Legal Assistance Office (JA), Pope AFB, OR 28308

Coast Guard: None

Legal Assistance for Servicemen Committee: Oregon State Bar, 4511 Southeast Hawthorne Boulevard, Portland, OR 97215; 503-235-8545

Pennsylvania

Marriage

Minimum age: male, 16; female, 16

Age requiring parental consent: male, under 18; female, under 18

Age not requiring parental consent: male, 18; female, 18

Blood-test requirement: yes

Waiting period: 3 days

Recognition of common-law marriage: yes

Grounds for divorce

Adultery

Bigamy

Blood relationship

Conviction of felony (for certain crimes involving a 2 year sentence)

Cruelty, physical

Desertion (2 years)

Duress of force

Fraud

Impotence at time of marriage

Insanity, postmarital (3 years)

Malformation preventing intercourse

Personal indignities (such as maliciously turning the wife out of doors)

Sterility

Grounds for legal separation

Abandonment

Adultery

Cruelty, physical

Personal indignities (such as maliciously turning the wife out of doors)

Grounds for annulment

Bigamy

Blood relationship

Insanity at time of marriage

Nonage

Grounds for declaring the marriage void

Bigamy

Residence requirement

1 year

What happens with inheritance if there is no will (intestacy)?

If there is one child, spouse inherits one-half. If there are no children, spouse inherits $2,000 of real or personal property and one-half of the remaining estate.

Note: No surviving spouse who had deserted and refused to support deceased spouse for 1 year prior to decedent's death can claim any right to the estate.

Other questions

Are holographic wills recognized? Yes

Can support (separate maintenance) for wife and

children be awarded from the time of filing for divorce until award of the final decree? Yes

Can alimony be awarded to take effect after the final decree? No

Can custody be awarded with the divorce (dissolution) decree? Yes

Can child support be awarded with the divorce (dissolution) decree? Yes

Are there dower rights? Yes

Can property be divided and awarded with the divorce (dissolution) decree? Yes

Is this a community property state? No

Can court allow wife to resume her former name? Yes

Is there a uniform reciprocal enforcement-of-support act? Yes

Legal Referral Service

Philadelphia, PA 19107: Philadelphia Bar Association, Suite 425, City Hall Annex; 215-686-5698

Pittsburgh, PA 15222: Allegheny County Bar Association, 920 City-County Building; 412-261-2088

Legal Aid

Philadelphia, PA 19107: Social Service Building, 3111 South Juniper Street; 215-735-6122

Pittsburgh, PA 15219: 200 Ross Street, Room 112; 412-261-6010

Armed Forces Legal Assistance

Army: Legal Assistance Office (SJA), U.S. Army Garrison, IGMR, Annville, PA 17003

Navy: Legal Assistance Officer, Naval Regional Medical Center, Philadelphia, PA 19145; 215-755-8311

Air Force: None

Coast Guard: None

Military Law Committee: Union County Bar Association, 36 South 32d Street, Lewisburg, PA 17837

Rhode Island

Marriage
    Minimum age: male, 18; female, 16
    Age requiring parental consent: male, under 18 cannot marry; female, under 18
    Age not requiring parental consent: male, 18; female, 18
    Blood-test requirement: yes
    Waiting period: none
    Recognition of common-law marriage: yes

Grounds for divorce
    Alcoholism
    Adultery
    Cruelty, physical (extreme)
    Desertion (5 years, or less at discretion of judge)
    Drug addiction
    Impotence at time of marriage
    No-fault (irreconcilable differences)
    Nonsupport (1 year)
    Other grounds (such as gross misbehavior of either party)
    Separation (3 years)

Grounds for legal separation
    Alcoholism
    Adultery
    Cruelty, physical (extreme)
    Desertion (5 years, or less at discretion of judge)
    Drug addiction
    Impotence
    Nonsupport
    Other grounds (such as gross misbehavior of either party)
    Separation (3 years)

Grounds for annulment
    Bigamy
    Blood relationship

Grounds for declaring the marriage void
    Bigamy

Blood relationship
Insanity
Nonage

Residence requirement
1 year

What happens with inheritance if there is no will (intestacy)?

If there are no children, the spouse inherits all realty, the first $50,000 of personal property, and one-half of the remainder. If there are children, surviving spouse inherits one-third of the real estate and one-half of the personal property.

Other questions
Are holographic wills recognized? No
Can support (separate maintenance) for wife and children be awarded from the time of filing for divorce until award of the final decree? Yes
Can alimony be awarded to take effect after the final decree? Yes
Can custody be awarded with the divorce (dissolution) decree? Yes
Can child support be awarded with the divorce (dissolution) decree? Yes
Are there dower rights? Yes
Can property be divided and awarded with the divorce (dissolution) decree? Yes
Is this a community property state? No
Can court allow wife to resume her former name? Yes
Is there a uniform reciprocal enforcement-of-support act? Yes

Legal Referral Service
Providence, RI 02903: Rhode Island Bar Association, 1804 Industrial Bank Building; 401-421-5740

Legal Aid
Providence, RI 02903: 76 Dorrance Street; 401-331-4665

Armed Forces Legal Assistance
Army: None

Navy: Legal Assistance Officer, Naval Legal Service
Office, Naval Education and Training Center,
Newport RI 02840; 401-841-3411
Air Force: None
Coast Guard: None

South Carolina

Marriage
Minimum age: male, 16; female, 14
Age requiring parental consent: male, under 18; female, under 18
Age not requiring parental consent: male, 18; female, 18
Blood-test requirement: no
Waiting period: 1 day
Recognition of common-law marriage: yes
Grounds for divorce
Adultery
Alcoholism
Cruelty, physical
Desertion (1 year)
Drug addiction
No-fault (separated for 1 year)
Separation (3 years)
Grounds for annulment
No real contract of marriage entered into
Grounds for declaring the marriage void
See grounds for annulment.
Residence requirement
1 year
What happens with inheritance if there is no will (intestacy)?
1. If widow has not waived her dower rights and there are no children and no relatives of the deceased (specified by South Carolina law), she inherits the entire estate.
2. If there are no children but decedent left relatives (specified by South Carolina law), surviving spouse inherits one-half of the entire estate.

3. If there is one child, surviving spouse inherits one-half of the entire estate.
4. If there is more than one child, surviving spouse inherits one-third of the entire estate.

Other questions

Are holographic wills recognized? No

Can support (separate maintenance) for wife and children be awarded from the time of filing for divorce until award of the final decree? Yes

Can alimony be awarded to take effect after the final decree? Yes (but wife's adultery cancels out alimony)

Can custody be awarded with the divorce (dissolution) decree? Yes

Can child support be awarded with the divorce (dissolution) decree? Yes

Are there dower rights? Yes

Can property be divided and awarded with the divorce (dissolution) decree? No

Is this a community property state? No

Can court allow wife to resume her former name? Yes

Is there a uniform reciprocal enforcement-of-support act? Yes

Legal Referral Service

Charleston, SC 29402: Charleston County Bar Association, P. O. Box 356; 803-723-3991

Legal Aid

Charleston, SC 29403: Neighborhood Legal Assistance Program, 119 Spring Street; 803-722-0107

Armed Forces Legal Assistance

Army: Legal Assistance Office, Office of the Staff Judge Advocate, Fort Jackson, SC 29207

Navy: Legal Assistance Officer, Naval Legal Service Office, Naval Base, Charleston, SC 29408; 803-743-4740

Air Force: Legal Assistance Office (JA), Charleston AFB, SC 29404

Coast Guard: None

South Dakota

Marriage
    Minimum age: male, 16; female, 16 (younger if she
        has or is expecting a child)
    Age requiring parental consent: male, under 18;
        female, under 18
    Age not requiring parental consent: male, 18; fe-
        male, 18
    Blood-test requirement: yes
    Waiting period: none
    Recognition of common-law marriage: no, unless
        consummated before July 1, 1959
Grounds for divorce
    Adultery
    Cruelty, mental (extreme)
    Cruelty, physical (extreme)
    Desertion
    Felony conviction
    Habitual intemperance (1 year)
    Willful neglect
Grounds for legal separation
    See grounds for divorce.
Grounds for annulment
    Bigamy
    Force or duress
    Fraud
    Impotence at time of marriage
    Insanity at time of marriage
    Malformation preventing intercourse (existent at
        time of marriage)
    Nonage
    Sterility at time of marriage
Grounds for declaring the marriage void
    Blood relationship
Residence requirement
    Ordinarily, 1 year. Six months if cause of action
        occurred in state. No requirement if parties mar-
        ried in the state and never left.

What happens with inheritance if there is no will (intestacy)?

1. If decedent leaves no issue and the estate does not exceed $100,000 in value, all the estate goes to surviving husband or wife.
2. If the estate exceeds $100,000, the first $100,000, goes to surviving husband or wife, who shall have the right of selecting the same; of all property in excess of $100,000 in value, one-half goes to surviving husband or wife, and the other half goes to decedent's father and mother in equal shares, and if either is dead the whole goes to the other, but if neither survives, such portion goes in equal shares to brothers and sisters of the decedent, and to children and grandchildren of any deceased brother or sister by right or representation.
3. If decedent leaves no issue, and no husband nor wife survives, the estate goes to decedent's father and mother in equal shares, or if either is dead, then to the other.

Other questions

Are holographic wills recognized? Yes

Can support (separate maintenance) for wife and children be awarded from the time of filing for divorce until award of the final decree? Yes

Can alimony be awarded to take effect after the final decree? Yes

Can custody be awarded with the divorce (dissolution) decree? Yes

Can child support be awarded with the divorce (dissolution) decree? Yes

Are there dower rights? No

Can property be divided and awarded with the divorce (dissolution) decree? Yes

Is this a community property state? No

Can court allow wife to resume her former name? Yes

Is there a uniform reciprocal enforcement-of-support act? Yes

Legal Referral Service

Aberdeen, SD 57401: Brown County Bar Association, County Clerk of Court's Office, P.O. Box 125; 605-225-1354

Sioux Falls, SD 57262: Legal Assistance Program, Minnehaha County

Legal Aid

Mission, SD 57555: South Dakota Legal Services Program, P.O. Box 148; 605-747-2241

Rapid City, SD 57701: Pennington County Bar Association, 300 West Boulevard

Armed Forces Legal Assistance

Army: None

Navy: Legal Assistance Officer, Naval Legal Service Office, Naval Training Center, Great Lakes, IL 60088; 312-688-3340

Air Force: Legal Assistance Office (JA), Ellsworth AFB, SD 57706; 605-688-3340

Coast Guard: None

Tennessee

Marriage

Minimum age: male, 16; female, 16

Age requiring parental consent: male, under 18; female, under 18

Age not requiring parental consent: male, 18; female, 18

Blood-test requirement: yes

Waiting period: 3 days

Recognition of common-law marriage: no

Grounds for divorce

Abandonment

Adultery

Alcoholism

Bigamy

Cruelty, mental

Cruelty, physical

Desertion (1 year)

Drug addiction

Felony conviction

Impotence

Irreconcilable differences

Nonsupport

Other grounds (such as attempted murder of spouse)

Personal indignities (only available as grounds to wife)

Pregnancy at the time of marriage without husband's knowledge

Wife's refusal to move with husband to the state of Tennessee (Applies under certain circumstances)

Grounds for legal separation

Abandonment

Cruelty, mental

Cruelty, physical

Nonsupport

Grounds for annulment

Bigamy

Blood relationship

Force or duress

Fraud

Insanity at time of marriage

Nonage

Grounds for declaring the marriage void

Bigamy

Blood relationship

Residence requirement

1 year

What happens with inheritance if there is no will (intestacy)?

If there are no children, surviving spouse inherits the entire estate. If there are children, surviving spouse inherits one-third of the estate.

Other questions

Are holographic wills recognized? Yes

Can support (separate maintenance) for wife and children be awarded from the time of filing for divorce until award of the final decree? Yes

Can alimony be awarded to take effect after the final decree? Yes

Can custody be awarded with the divorce (dissolution) decree? Yes

Can child support be awarded with the divorce (dissolution) decree? Yes

Are there dower rights? No

Can property be divided and awarded with the divorce (dissolution) decree? Yes

Is this a community property state? No

Can court allow wife to resume her former name? Yes

Is there a uniform reciprocal enforcement-of-support act? Yes

Legal Referral Service

Memphis, TN 38103: Memphis and Shelby County Bar Association, 200 Court House; 901-527-6002

Nashville, TN 37201: Nashville Bar Association, 327 Stahlman Building; 615-242-6546, 615-242-6547

Legal Aid

Knoxville, TN 37916: Legal Aid Clinic, University of Tennessee, College of Law, 1505 West Cumberland Avenue; 615-174-2331

Memphis, TN 38103: Memphis and Shelby County Bar Association, 200 Court House; 901-527-9342

Armed Forces Legal Assistance

Army: None

Navy: Legal Assistance Officer, Naval Legal Service Office, Naval Air Station Memphis, Millington, TN 38054; 901-872-5308

Air Force: Legal Assistance Office (JA), Arnold Engineering Development Center, Arnold Air Force Station, TN 37389

Coast Guard: None

Texas

Marriage

Minimum age: male, 16; female, 16

Age requiring parental consent: male, under 18; female, under 18

Age not requiring parental consent: male, 18; female, 18

Blood-test requirement: yes

Waiting period: none

Recognition of common-law marriage: yes

Grounds for divorce

Abandonment (1 year)

Adultery

Cruelty, mental

Cruelty, physical

Felony conviction (1 year after conviction, provided that one spouse did not testify against the other and that convicted spouse is not pardoned)

Insanity, postmarital (3 years confinement in a mental institution)

No-fault (when marriage becomes insupportable with no reasonable expectation of reconciliation)

Separation (3 years)

Grounds for legal separation

There is no legal separation in this state, but if a couple is living apart, either can sue for custody without suing for divorce.

Grounds for annulment

Blood relationship

Impediment that renders the marital contract void

Impotence at time of marriage

Grounds for declaring the marriage void

Blood relationship

Residence requirement

6 months in state and 90 days in county where suit is filed

What happens with inheritance if there is no will (intestacy)?

1. If there are children, surviving spouse inherits one-third of the separate property.

2. If deceased left no children, but left relatives specified by Texas law, spouse inherits one-half of the separate property.

3. If there are none of the aforementioned relatives, spouse inherits the entire estate.

4. All community property goes to spouse if there are no children.
5. If there are children, spouse is entitled to one-half of the community estate.

Other questions

Are holographic wills recognized? Yes

Can support (separate maintenance) for wife and children be awarded from the time of filing for divorce until award of the final decree? Yes

Can alimony be awarded to take effect after the final decree? No. (But parties can agree that one will make periodic payments to the other as part of a separation agreement.)

Can custody be awarded with the divorce (dissolution) decree? Yes

Can child support be awarded with the divorce (dissolution) decree? Yes

Are there dower rights? No

Can property be divided and awarded with the divorce (dissolution) decree? Yes

Is this a community property state? Yes

Can court allow either party to resume former name? Yes

Is there a uniform reciprocal enforcement-of-support act? Yes

Legal Referral Service

Austin, TX 78711: State Bar of Texas, P.O. Box 12487; 512-476-6823

Legal Aid

Austin, TX 78767: Legal Aid and Defender, Society of Travis County (Legal Aid Office), 1713 East 6th Street; 512-476-6321

Dallas, TX 75202: 502 States General Life Building, 708 Jackson Street

Houston, TX 77002: Houston Legal Foundation, Legal Aid and Defender Office, Suite 1909, 609 Fannin Building; 713-225-0321

San Antonio, TX 78207: Bexar County Legal Aid Association, 203 West Nueva Street; 512-227-0111

Armed Forces Legal Assistance

Army: Legal Assistance Officer, HQ 5th Army, Fort Sam Houston, TX 78234

Navy: Legal Assistance Officer, Naval Air Station, Kingsville, TX 78363; 512-592-4361, ext. 412

Air Force: Legal Assistance Officer, Brooks AFB, TX 78743

Coast Guard: None

Military Liaison Committee: Abilene Bar Association, P.O. Box 1, Abilene, TX 79604

Utah

Marriage

Minimum age: male, 14; female, 14

Age requiring parental consent: male, under 18; female, under 18

Age not requiring parental consent: male, 18; female, 18

Blood-test requirement: yes

Waiting period: none

Recognition of common-law marriage: no

Grounds for divorce

Adultery

Alcoholism

Cruelty, mental

Cruelty, physical

Desertion (1 year)

Felony conviction

Impotence at time of marriage

Insanity, postmarital

Neglect, willful

No-fault (separation for 3 years)

Nonsupport

Grounds for legal separation

Desertion (1 year)

Nonsupport

Grounds for annulment

Bigamy

Common-law grounds

Force or duress
Fraud
Nonage
Venereal disease

Grounds for declaring the marriage void

Bigamy
Blood relationship
Marriage not solemnized by proper authority (if consummated in belief there was authority, marriage is valid)
Venereal disease

Residence requirement

3 months

What happens with inheritance if there is no will (intestacy)?

1. If there are no surviving parents or children of deceased, surviving spouse inherits the entire estate.
2. If there are no surviving children, but parents of deceased are living, the remaining spouse inherits $100,000 and one-half of the balance of the estate.
3. If there are children of surviving spouse, spouse inherits the first $50,000 and one-half of the balance of the estate.
4. If there are children one or more of whom are not issue of surviving spouse, spouse inherits one-half of the estate.

Other questions

Are holographic wills recognized? Yes
Can support (separate maintenance) for wife and children be awarded from the time of filing for divorce until award of the final decree? Yes
Can alimony be awarded to take effect after the final decree? Yes
Can custody be awarded with the divorce (dissolution) decree? Yes
Can child support be awarded with the divorce (dissolution) decree? Yes
Are there dower rights? No
Can property be divided and awarded with the divorce (dissolution) decree? Yes
Is this a community property state? No

Can court allow wife to resume her former name?
Yes

Is there a uniform reciprocal enforcement-of-support act? Yes

Legal Referral Service

Salt Lake City, UT 84111: Utah Bar Association, 425 East 1st S; 801-322-5273

Legal Aid

Salt Lake City, UT 84111: Utah Legal Services, 216 East 5th S; 801-328-8891

Salt Lake City, UT 84101: 314 Atlas Building; 801-328-8849

Armed Forces Legal Assistance

Army: Legal Assistance Officer, Office of the Staff Judge Advocate, Tooele Army Depot, UT 84075

Navy: Legal Assistance Office, Naval Legal Service Office, Treasure Island, San Francisco, CA 94130; 415-765-5287

Air Force: Legal Assistance Office (JA), Hill AFB, UT 84406

Coast Guard: None

Vermont

Marriage

Minimum age: male, 16; female, 16

Age requiring parental consent: male, under 18; female, under 18

Age not requiring parental consent: male, 18; female, 18

Blood-test requirement: yes

Waiting period: 5 days

Recognition of common-law marriage: no

Grounds for divorce

Abandonment

Adultery

Cruelty, mental (intolerable severity)

Cruelty, physical (intolerable severity)

Desertion (6 months)

Felony conviction

Imprisonment

Insanity, postmarital (5 years)

No-fault (living apart for 6 months with court finding resumption of marital relations not probable)

Nonsupport

Grounds for legal separation

Adultery

Desertion (6 months)

Felony conviction

Insanity, postmarital (5 years)

No-fault (separation for 6 months)

Nonsupport

Grounds for annulment

Bigamy

Blood relationship

Force or duress

Fraud

Impotence

Insanity at time of marriage

Marriage not solemnized by proper authority

Nonage

Venereal disease

Grounds for declaring the marriage void

Bigamy

Blood relationship

Residence requirement

6 months

What happens with inheritance if there is no will (intestacy)?

If there are no children, surviving spouse inherits up to $25,000 of the estate. If there is one child, spouse inherits one-half of the estate. If there is more than one child, spouse inherits one-third of the estate.

Other questions

Are holographic wills recognized? No

Can support (separate maintenance) for wife and children be awarded from the time of filing for divorce until award of the final decree? Yes

Can alimony be awarded to take effect after the final decree? Yes

Can custody be awarded with the divorce (dissolution) decree? Yes

Can child support be awarded with the divorce (dissolution) decree? Yes

Are there dower rights? Yes

Can property be divided and awarded with the divorce (dissolution) decree? Yes

Is this a community property state? No

Can court allow wife to resume her former name? Yes

Is there a uniform reciprocal enforcement-of-support act? Yes

Legal Referral Service

Montpelier, VT 05602: Vermont Bar Association, P.O. Box 100; 800-642-3153

Legal Aid

Montpelier, VT 05602: 52 State Street, Box 658; 802-223-6306

Armed Forces Legal Assistance

Army: None

Navy: Legal Assistance Office, Headquarters 1st Naval District, 495 Summer Street, Boston, MA 02110

Air Force: None

Coast Guard: None

Virginia

Marriage

Minimum age: male, 16; female, 16

Age requiring parental consent: male, under 18; female, under 18

Age not requiring parental consent: male, 18; female, 18

Blood-test requirement: yes

Waiting period: none

Recognition of common-law marriage: no (unless created in another state)

Grounds for divorce

Abandonment (1 year)

Adultery

Crime against nature

Desertion, cruelty, or reasonable apprehension of bodily hurt (1 year: constructive)

Felony conviction (imprisoned for more than 1 year)

No-fault (separation for 1 year)

Grounds for legal separation

Abandonment

Cruelty, mental

Cruelty, physical

Desertion

Reasonable fear of bodily harm

Grounds for annulment

Bigamy

Blood relationship

Force or duress

Fraud

Impotence at time of marriage

Insanity at time of marriage

Malformation preventing intercourse

Marriage not solemnized by proper authority

Nonage

Other grounds (such as no knowledge that spouse was convicted of a felony or was a prostitute before marriage)

Wife's pregnancy by another man or husband's fatherhood with another woman at time of marriage

Note: There is a 2-year statute of limitations from the date of marriage.

Grounds for declaring the marriage void

Mental incapacity or infirmity

Grounds for declaring the marriage void without decree

Bigamy

Blood relationship

Residence requirement

6 months

What happens with inheritance if there is no will (intestacy)?

If there are no children, surviving spouse inherits the entire estate. If there are children, surviving spouse

inherits one-third of the personal property and one-
third "fee simple absolute" in real property.

Other questions

Are holographic wills recognized? Yes

Can support (separate maintenance) for wife and
children be awarded from the time of filing for
divorce until award of the final decree? Yes

Can alimony be awarded to take effect after the
final decree? Yes

Can custody be awarded with the divorce (dissolution) decree? Yes

Can child support be awarded with the divorce (dissolution) decree? Yes

Are there dower rights? Yes

Can property be divided and awarded with the divorce (dissolution) decree? Yes

Is this a community property state? No

Can court allow wife to resume her former name? Yes

Is there a uniform reciprocal enforcement-of-support act? Yes

Legal Aid

Norfolk, VA 23510: Tidewater Legal Aid Society,
William E. Fulford, Director, 147 Granby Street,
Room 350; 804-627-5423

Richmond, VA 23219: Robert Metcalf, Director,
18 North 8th Street; 804-648-2821

Branch offices: Alexandria, Arlington, Charlottes-
ville, Christiansburg, Fairfax, Fredericksburg,
Harrisonburg, Lynchburg, Marion, Petersburg,
Portsmouth, Roanoke, Staunton, Waynesboro,
Woodbridge, VA

Armed Forces Legal Assistance

Army: Legal Assistance Officer, U.S.A. Engineer,
Fort Belvoir, VA 22060

Navy: Legal Assistance Officer, Naval Legal Service
Office, Naval Base, Norfolk, VA 23511; 804-444-
7561

Air Force: Legal Assistance Office (JA), 4638 Air
Defense Squadron, Fort Lee Air Force Station,
VA 23801

Coast Guard: Legal Assistance Officer, c/o Commander 5th Coast District (DL), Federal Building, 431 Crawford Street, Portsmouth, VA 23705; 804-393-9611, exts. 361, 362

Washington

Marriage
Minimum age: male, 17; female, 17
Age requiring parental consent: male, under 18; female, under 18
Age not requiring parental consent: male, 18; female, 18
Blood-test requirement: no
Waiting period: 3 days
Recognition of common-law marriage: no
Grounds for divorce
Abandonment (1 year)
Adultery
Consent obtained by force or fraud
Cruelty
Drunkenness (habitual)
Impotence
Imprisonment
Insanity (2 years)
Lack of capacity to consent
No-fault (irretrievable breakdown)
Nonsupport by husband
Separation (5 years)
Grounds for legal separation
No-fault (irretrievable breakdown)
Grounds for declaring the marriage void
Bigamy
Blood relationship
Force or duress
Fraud
Lack of capacity to consent
Nonage
Refusal to cohabit
Residence requirement
None

What happens with inheritance if there is no will (intestacy)?

Surviving spouse receives (1) All the decedent's share of the net community estate; and (2) one-half of the net separate estate if intestate is survived by issue; or (3) three-fourths of the net separate estate if there is no surviving issue, but intestate is survived by one or more of his parents, or by one or more of the issue of one or more of his parents; (4) all of the net separate estate, if there is no surviving issue or parents or issue of parents.

Other questions

Are holographic wills recognized? No

Can support (separate maintenance) for wife and children be awarded from the time of filing for divorce until award of the final decree? Yes

Can maintenance be awarded to take effect after the final decree? Yes

Can custody be awarded with the divorce (dissolution) decree? Yes

Can child support be awarded with the divorce (dissolution) decree? Yes

Are there dower rights? No

Can property be divided and awarded with the divorce (dissolution) decree? Yes

Is this a community property state? Yes

Can court allow wife to resume her former name? Yes

Is there a uniform reciprocal enforcement-of-support act? Yes

Legal Referral Service

Seattle, WA 98104: Washington State Bar Association, 505 Madison Street; 206-622-6054

Legal Aid

Seattle, WA 98104: Legal Services Center, 2516 East Cherry Street; 206-464-5941

Spokane, WA 99201: Spokane Legal Services Center, 246 Riverside Avenue W; 509-838-3671

Armed Forces Legal Assistance

Army: Legal Assistance Office (JA), HQ 9th Infantry Division, Fort Lewis, WA 98433

Navy: Legal Assistance Officer, Naval Legal Service Office, Seattle, WA 98115; 206-527-3835

Air Force: Office of the Staff Judge Advocate, Building 524, McChord AFB, WA 98438

Coast Guard: Legal Assistance Officer, c/o Commander 13th Coast Guard District (BL), 915 2d Avenue, Seattle, WA 98174; 206-442-5295

West Virginia

Marriage
    Minimum age: male, none; female, none
    Age requiring parental consent: male, no minimum; female, no minimum
    Age not requiring parental consent: male, 18; female, 18
    Blood-test requirement: yes
    Waiting period: 3 days
    Recognition of common-law marriage: no
Grounds for divorce
    Abandonment (1 year)
    Adultery
    Alcoholism
    Cruelty, mental
    Cruelty, physical
    Desertion (1 year)
    Drug addiction
    Felony conviction
    Insanity, postmarital (3 years)
    No-fault (separation for 2 years)
Grounds for annulment
    Bigamy
    Blood relationship
    Force or duress
    Fraud
    Impotence
    Insanity at time of marriage
    Malformation preventing intercourse

Nonage

Other grounds (such as either party epileptic at marriage; no knowledge that spouse was convicted of infamous offense before marriage; no knowledge that wife was prostitute before marriage; no knowledge that husband was notoriously licentious before marriage)

Pregnancy (see page 128)

Venereal disease at time of marriage

Grounds for declaring the marriage void

See grounds for annulment.

Residence requirement

1 year (none for adultery)

What happens with inheritance if there is no will (intestacy)?

If there are no children, surviving spouse inherits the entire estate. If there are children, surviving spouse inherits one-third of the estate.

Other questions

Are holographic wills recognized? Yes

Can support (separate maintenance) for wife and children be awarded from the time of filing for divorce until award of the final decree? Yes

Can alimony be awarded to take effect after the final decree? Yes

Can custody be awarded with the divorce (dissolution) decree? Yes

Can child support be awarded with the divorce (dissolution) decree? Yes

Are there dower rights? Yes

Can property be divided and awarded with the divorce (dissolution) decree? Yes

Is this a community property state? No

Can court allow wife to resume her former name? Yes

Is there a uniform reciprocal enforcement-of-support act? Yes

Legal Referral Service

No state or local Legal Referral Services

Legal Aid

Charleston, WV 25305: West Virginia Legal Service Plan, Room W-127, State Capitol; 304-348-8980

Armed Forces Legal Assistance
Army: None
Navy: Legal Assistance Officer, Naval Legal Service Office, Naval Base, Norfolk, VA 23511; 804-444-7561
Air Force: None
Coast Guard: None

Wisconsin

Marriage
Minimum age: male, 16; female, 16
Age requiring parental consent: male, under 18; female, under 18
Age not requiring parental consent: male, 18; female, 18
Blood-test requirement: yes
Waiting period: 5 days
Recognition of common-law marriage: no
Grounds for divorce
Adultery
Alcoholism (1 year)
Cruelty, mental
Cruelty, physical
Desertion (1 year)
Felony conviction (committed to prison for 3 years)
Impotence
Irretrievable breakdown of marriage
Separation, voluntary (5 years)
Grounds for legal separation
See grounds for divorce.
Grounds for annulment
Bigamy
Blood relationship
Force or duress
Fraud
Impotence
Insanity at time of marriage

Malformation preventing intercourse
Marriage within 1 year after previous divorce
Nonage

Grounds for declaring the marriage void
Bigamy
Blood relationship
Marriage not properly solemnized
Nonage

Residence requirement
6 months

What happens with inheritance if there is no will (intestacy)?

If there are no children, surviving spouse inherits the entire estate. If there is one child, spouse inherits $25,000 and one-half of the balance of the estate. If there is more than one child, spouse inherits $25,000 and one-third of the balance of the estate.

Other questions
Are holographic wills recognized? No
Can support (separate maintenance) for wife and children be awarded from the time of filing for divorce until award of the final decree? Yes
Can alimony be awarded to take effect after the final decree? Yes
Can custody be awarded with the divorce (dissolution) decree? Yes
Can child support be awarded with the divorce (dissolution) decree? Yes
Are there dower rights Yes
Can property be divided and awarded with the divorce (dissolution) decree? Yes
Is this a community property state? No
Can court allow wife to resume her former name? Yes
Is there a uniform reciprocal enforcement-of-support act? Yes

Legal Referral Service
Madison, WI 53703: Dane County Bar Association, 402 West Wilson Street; 608-257-2866
Milwaukee, WI 53202: Milwaukee Bar Association, 740 North Plankinton Avenue; 414-271-3080

Legal Aid

Madison, WI 53702: Howard B. Eisenberg, State Public Defender, 123 West Washington Avenue; 608-266-3440

Milwaukee, WI 53202: Milwaukee Legal Services, Inc., 211 West Kilbourn Avenue

Armed Forces Legal Assistance

Army: None

Navy: Legal Assistance Officer, Naval Legal Service Office, Naval Training Center, Great Lakes, IL 60088; 312-688-3340

Air Force: None

Coast Guard: None

Wyoming

Marriage

Minimum age: male, 18; female, 16

Age requiring parental consent: male, under 19; female, under 19

Age not requiring parental consent: male, 19; female, 19

Blood-test requirement: yes

Waiting period: none

Recognition of common-law marriage: no

Grounds for divorce

Adultery

Alcoholism

Cruelty, mental (extreme)

Cruelty, physical (extreme)

Desertion (1 year)

Felony conviction

Impotence at time of marriage

Insanity, postmarital (2 years)

Irreconcilable differences (corroboration by another witness required)

Malformation preventing intercourse

Nonsupport

Personal indignities

Pregnancy at time of marriage

Separation (2 years)
Vagrancy, husband's

Grounds for legal separation
Adultery
Alcoholism
Cruelty, mental (extreme)
Cruelty, physical (extreme)
Desertion (1 year)
Felony conviction
Insanity, postmarital (2 years)
Nonsupport
Personal indignities
Separation (2 years)

Grounds for annulment
Bigamy
Blood relationship
Force or duress
Fraud
Impotence at time of marriage
Insanity at time of marriage
Malformation preventing intercourse
Nonage
Venereal disease

Grounds for declaring the marriage void
Bigamy
Blood relationship
Insanity at time of marriage
Venereal disease

Residence requirement
60 days

What happens with inheritance if there is no will (intestacy)?
If there are no children, surviving spouse inherits the entire estate. If there are children, surviving spouse inherits one-half of the estate.

Other questions
Are holographic wills recognized? Yes
Can support (separate maintenance) for wife and children be awarded from the time of filing for divorce until award of the final decree? Yes

Can alimony be awarded to take effect after the final decree? Yes

Can custody be awarded with the divorce (dissolution) decree? Yes

Can child support be awarded with the divorce (dissolution) decree? Yes

Are there dower rights? No

Can property be divided and awarded with the divorce (dissolution) decree? Yes

Is this a community property state? No

Can court allow wife to resume her former name? Yes

Is there a uniform reciprocal enforcement-of-support act? Yes

Legal Referral Service

No state or local Legal Referral Services

Legal Aid

Cheyenne, WY 82001: Laramie County Legal Service, 1810 Pioneer Avenue; 307-634-1566

Armed Forces Legal Assistance

Army: None

Navy: Legal Assistance Officer, Naval Legal Service Office, Naval Training Center, Great Lakes, IL 60088; 312-688-3340

Air Force: Legal Assistance Office (JA), Frances E. Warren AFB, WY 82001; 307-775-3811, 307-775-3420, 307-775-3421

Coast Guard: None

District of Columbia

Marriage

Minimum age: male, 16; female, 16

Age requiring parental consent: male, under 18; female, under 18

Age not requiring parental consent: male, 18; female, 18

Blood-test requirement: yes

Waiting period: 3 days

Recognition of common-law marriage: yes

Grounds for divorce
No-fault (separation for 1 year)
Voluntary separation (6 months)

Grounds for legal separation
Adultery
Cruelty, mental
Cruelty, physical
Separation (1 year)
Voluntary separation (6 months)

Grounds for annulment
Bigamy
Fraud or coercion
Insanity at time of marriage
Matrimonial incapacity
Nonage

Grounds for declaring the marriage void
Bigamy
Blood relationship

Residence requirement
1 year

What happens with inheritance if there is no will (intestacy)?

If widow has not waived her dower rights and there are no children or grandchildren, she inherits the entire estate. If there are no descendants but parents of the deceased, spouse inherits one-half of the estate. If there are children or grandchildren, spouse inherits one-third of the estate.

Other questions
Are holographic wills recognized? Yes, but must be signed by testator and attested and subscribed to by at least two witnesses
Can support (separate maintenance) for wife and children be awarded from the time of filing for divorce until award of the final decree? Yes
Can alimony be awarded to take effect after the final decree? Yes
Can custody be awarded with the divorce (dissolution) decree? Yes

Can child support be awarded with the divorce (dissolution) decree? Yes

Are there dower rights? Yes

Can property be divided and awarded with the divorce (dissolution) decree? Yes

Is this a community property state? No

Can court allow wife to resume her former name? Yes

Is there a uniform reciprocal enforcement-of-support act? Yes

Legal Referral Service

Washington, DC 20006: 1819 H Street, NW; 202-223-1484

Legal Aid

Washington, DC 20001: Suite 300, 666 11th Street, NW; 202-628-1161

Armed Forces Legal Assistance

Army: Walter Reed Army Medical Center, Forest Glen Section, Washington, DC 20012

Navy: Legal Assistance Officer, Naval Legal Service Office, Washington Navy Yard, Washington, DC 20374; 202-433-4331

Air Force: Legal Assistance Office (JA), Room 100C, Building P-20, Bolling AFB, Washington, DC 20332

Coast Guard: Legal Assistance Officer, U.S. Coast Guard (G-LLA/84), 400 7th Street, SW, Washington, D.C. 20590; 202-426-2256

Puerto Rico

Marriage

Minimum age: male, 18; female, 16*

Age requiring parental consent: male, 14; female, 14*

Age not requiring parental consent: male, 18; female, 16*

---

*These ages do not apply in cases of seduction and/or pregnancy.

Blood-test requirement: medical certificate required
Waiting period: none
Recognition of common-law marriage: no

Grounds for divorce

Abandonment (1 year)

Adultery

Attempt of husband or wife to corrupt their sons or prostitute their daughters (or connivance in such corruption or prostitution)

Conviction of a felony that may involve the loss of civil rights

Cruel treatment or grave injury

Habitual drunkenness or continued and excessive use of drugs

Impotence occurring after marriage (absolute, perpetual, and incurable)

Insanity, incurable (of either spouse for more than 7 years when it "seriously prevents spouses from living together spiritually")

Proposal of husband to prostitute his wife

Separation (more than 2 years, uninterrupted)

Grounds for legal separation or annulment

There is no statutory provision for legal separation or annulment.

Residence requirement

1 year for plaintiff; none for defendant

What happens with inheritance if there is no will (intestacy)?

Proportions determined by a superior court (1) to direct descendants; (2) to descendants; (3) to brothers or sisters and their descendants; (4) to surviving spouse; (5) to collaterals up to the sixth degree; (6) to the University of Puerto Rico.

Note: Even if there is a will, inheritance goes to certain heirs by clan, called forced heirs.

Other questions

Are holographic wills recognized? Yes

Can support (separate maintenance) for wife and children be awarded from the time of filing for divorce until award of the final decree? Yes

Can alimony be awarded to take effect after the final decree? Yes

Can custody be awarded with the divorce (dissolution) decree? Yes

Can child support be awarded with the divorce (dissolution) decree? Yes

Are there dower rights? No

Can property be divided and awarded with the divorce (dissolution) decree? Yes

Is this a community property state? Yes

Can court allow wife to resume her former name? No

Is there a uniform reciprocal enforcement-of-support act? Yes

Legal Aid and Defender Offices

Aguadilla, PR 00603: Sociedad para Asistencia, Legal Branch, Calle Progreso No. 69; 800-891-2030

Humacao, PR 00661: Sociedad para Asistencia, Legal Branch, Calle Esbrella No. 28; 764-842-3172

Rio Piedras, PR 00928: Legal Aid Clinic, School of Law, University of Puerto Rico; 764-0000E569

Armed Forces Legal Assistance

No statutes

Postscript

This book was designed to help you cope with the problems of marriage and divorce under the existing conditions. I tried not to be too critical of our present system of family law.

My next book will propose programs to help restore the family as the backbone of our societal structure. The deterioration of the family as our primary social unit continues because parents are not doing the job, schools are not doing the job, religious institutions are not doing the job, politicians are not doing the job, and psychiatrists, psychologists, and so on, seem to need more help than they provide.

In this century, during which the United States has participated in four wars, the battleground has been established and the initial skirmishes have already taken place in another war: the battle of the sexes.

Within a few months of announcing my concern about marriage and divorce problems, I received many calls and letters from a variety of men's rights groups. I was already aware of the feminist movement, having met some of its leading spokespersons. Now I can assure you that for every fervent feminist there is a maniacal "masculinist," one of a breed of men who blame women for every masculine failure since the beginning of our species. They quote books, from the Bible to contemporary literature. They try to prove that American men have precipitated wars in order to prove a masculinity which had been diminished by American women. The vitriolic tone of their rantings is alarming.

Extremists of both sexes are helping tear our society apart.

Lawrence Van Gelder, a concerned writer for the family section of *The New York Times,* quoted me on September 21, 1976, as follows: "I think in the high schools of America there should be a mandatory course on the dangers and perils of marriage and divorce. This subject is much more important than Greek and Latin to the average American student. If it were taught in a practical way, so that the students realized what they were up against before they married impetuously and immediately had children only to be left alone to support them a few years later, it is possible there would be more enlightenment and less suffering."

I am preparing a textbook for use in such a course.

Even if we can reduce the divorce rate, our societal structure has already been reshaped so that the fatherless or motherless home has become a way of life for a huge segment of the population. Our children have not been educated to accept this, and something must be done to orient them. Beginning in high school, proper instruction may help them adjust and, let's hope, avoid unwise marriages themselves.

But orientation on marriage and divorce can begin before high school. With the use of television shows, books, comics, and films imaginatively produced for children in nursery and grammar schools, future generations can be educated to accept without trauma their single-parent family unit as well as the possibility of new mothers and fathers entering their lives, without the antagonism that is now so prevalent.

I will also propose a new basis for temporary spousal support and child support. As soon as a spouse fails to perform as a husband or wife, and separates or sues for dissolution of the marriage, mandatory payments based on gross income and the number of children will take effect. These temporary spousal- and child-support payments would afford a reasonable minimum not so high as to increase separation and divorce rates. Some of the financial, emotional, and physical strain of separation and divorce would be eliminated along with the strain of uncertainty. I believe that knowing more about what you would receive could lessen the divorce rate rather than increase it.

Our current system is the adversary system in which there is no longer meaningful law, but only lawyers and judges who use what is euphemistically called their discretion. There has to be a better way. If my guidelines for support are adopted, there will be less need for the legal battles that embitter the parties to so many divorces, since both parties would know in advance about what to expect upon divorce.

My program, if instituted on a national scale, would save much of the expense of the adversary system. Judges would use guidelines rather than being forced to spend hours supervising legal battles, and might no longer be needed to handle routine alimony matters. Their time could be devoted to types of litigation that really call for the services of legal experts.

Too many wives assume that marriage entitles them to one-half of their marital domiciles, but don't get their half. With my program each spouse will automatically receive half ownership in the home. I will offer national guidelines for custody hearings on the premise that children are more important than parents in custody proceedings. No solution to this tragic problem is going to be completely satisfactory; but anything that will ease the hurt will improve on our present chaotic custody procedures.

During the Great Depression of the thirties, Dr. Francis Townsend proposed the Townsend Plan of $200 monthly pensions for the old. Many people called him a crazy reformer, but our social security system resulted in part from his efforts.

Six years ago, Diana Du Broff, a family law attorney, was inspired to coin the phrase "divorce insurance." She has not yet received the national publicity that Dr. Townsend got. In my opinion, divorce insurance for child support is the only reasonable solution to the problems now being faced by millions of newly separated families with children.

One of the most tragic situations in America is the mother left with infants and barely enough money to survive. She is forced to depend upon governments —local, state, and federal—for help. If this help comes, it is limited. Many of us have witnessed the shame and humiliation to which such unfortunate mothers are subjected.

Fathers, too, have problems. They are bitter when they are not awarded custody and have to make monthly payments to estranged wives. They find visiting their children in their ex-wife's domicile most unpleasant.

The greater the financial and economic security the less the emotional and physical insecurity. This thought is the basis for my work in the field of marriage and divorce.

In my plan of divorce insurance, parents who are not separated or divorced would pay premiums which would be used for child-support payments to the separated or divorced parent with custody, so that the parent can continue raising the children without resorting to charity or welfare.

Hiring baby-sitters while she works is often too expensive for the mother left alone with young children. To relieve millions of working mothers of this burden, I propose a national chain of day-care centers. Model day-care centers can be organized using input from those who are already successful in this field, supported by sociologists, educators, and so on.

Here is a way to reduce the cost of land and buildings for day-care centers. In every neighborhood in the country, tax-free facilities, such as churches, synagogues, recreational facilities would be used as day-care centers during hours and days when they would otherwise be closed. Thousands of unused rooms could be used with the stipulation that there would be no interference with normal religious activities. This would be in the spirit of the present powerful trend to eliminate the tax-free aspects of religious activities. Also, those using the land and buildings would pay their share—and perhaps a little more—of the expenses of maintaining the facilities.

Day-care employment can be offered to the elderly and those unable to afford transportation to distant employment, in centers close to their homes, especially in and near large housing projects. Professionals agree that adults will more lovingly and attentively monitor the activities of little ones in their neighborhoods.

My next land development, now in the planning stage, envisions 1000 housing units for low-income people, plus a day-care center. I expect to learn by trial and error whether my proposal has any merit, and hope to make my point through example.

All these proposals are subject to extensive research and modification. No program taken alone can be as effective as several of them coordinated.

The programs will probably provide a field day for detractors—those who never offer anything constructive, who can always tell us why things are impossible. We cannot afford to listen to them.

I see a great need for constant communication with the millions of people who have problems in dating, marriage, and divorce, and who want accurate and unbiased information.

In addition to speaking up in the media, I am writing another book as an outgrowth of my research and experiences. It will be called *Public Enemy Number One—Lawyers and Judges*.

I have little faith in the professional who performs for money. His work is necessarily colored by his desire for profit. Granted, there are times when one can do good and make money at the same time, but moneymaking can easily become primary.

It is gratifying, however, to see that more than a hundred concerned lawyers, judges, legislators, educators, psychiatrists, and people from all walks of life have called and written me, offering to participate in a national crusade to find practical solutions to the problems discussed in this book.

I need suggestions, advice, and encouragement from everyone. So—write me.

If after synthesizing, refining, and detailing this blueprint for the future I feel that the goals are attainable, I will finance a national convention for their implementation, inviting individuals and groups to participate.

Let us work toward the day when this blueprint for the future evolves into workable solutions of the present!

Index

ABOUT THE AUTHOR

DAVID I. LEVINE, a native of Norfolk, Virginia, is one of Virginia's largest land developers. He has an A.B. in economics from George Washington University. He has taught seminars at Old Dominion University and has lectured at the Wharton School of Finance and Commerce of the University of Pennsylvania. Mr. Levine has spent thirty and one half years of his life as a married man. He has spent the last three years becoming an expert on divorce.

RELAX!
SIT DOWN
and Catch Up On Your Reading!

☐	11877	**HOLOCAUST** by Gerald Green	$2.25
☐	12836	**THE CHANCELLOR MANUSCRIPT** by Robert Ludlum	$2.75
☐	12859	**TRINITY** by Leon Uris	$2.95
☐	2300	**THE MONEYCHANGERS** by Arthur Hailey	$1.95
☐	12550	**THE MEDITERRANEAN CAPER** by Clive Cussler	$2.25
☐	11469	**AN EXCHANGE OF EAGLES** by Owen Sela	$2.25
☐	2600	**RAGTIME** by E. L. Doctorow	$2.25
☐	11428	**FAIRYTALES** by Cynthia Freeman	$2.25
☐	11966	**THE ODESSA FILE** by Frederick Forsyth	$2.25
☐	11557	**BLOOD RED ROSES** by Elizabeth B. Coker	$2.25
☐	11708	**JAWS 2** by Hank Searls	$2.25
☐	12490	**TINKER, TAILOR, SOLDIER, SPY** by John Le Carre	$2.50
☐	11929	**THE DOGS OF WAR** by Frederick Forsyth	$2.25
☐	10526	**INDIA ALLEN** by Elizabeth B. Coker	$1.95
☐	12489	**THE HARRAD EXPERIMENT** by Robert Rimmer	$2.25
☐	11767	**IMPERIAL 109** by Richard Doyle	$2.50
☐	10500	**DOLORES** by Jacqueline Susann	$1.95
☐	11601	**THE LOVE MACHINE** by Jacqueline Susann	$2.25
☐	11886	**PROFESSOR OF DESIRE** by Philip Roth	$2.50
☐	12433	**THE DAY OF THE JACKAL** by Frederick Forsyth	$2.50
☐	11952	**DRAGONARD** by Rupert Gilchrist	$1.95
☐	11331	**THE HAIGERLOCH PROJECT** by Ib Melchior	$2.25
☐	11330	**THE BEGGARS ARE COMING** by Mary Loos	$1.95

Buy them at your local bookstore or use this handy coupon for ordering:

WE DELIVER!
And So Do These Bestsellers.

How's Your Health?

Bantam publishes a line of informative books, written by top experts to help you toward a healthier and happier life.

☐	10350	**DR. ATKINS' SUPERENERGY DIET,** Robert Atkins, M.D.	$2.25
☐	12719	**FASTING: The Ultimate Diet,** Allan Cott, M.D.	$1.95
☐	12762	**WEIGHT CONTROL THROUGH YOGA** Richard Hittleman	$1.95
☐	11872	**A DICTIONARY OF SYMPTOMS,** Gomez	$2.25
☐	13000	**THE BRAND NAME NUTRITION COUNTER,** Jean Carper	$2.25
☐	12607	**SWEET AND DANGEROUS,** John Yudkin, M.D.	$2.25
☐	12362	**NUTRITION AGAINST DISEASE,** Roger J. Williams	$2.25
☐	12174	**NUTRITION AND YOUR MIND,** George Watson	$2.25
☐	12360	**THE NEW AEROBICS,** Kenneth Cooper, M.D.	$2.25
☐	12468	**AEROBICS FOR WOMEN,** Kenneth Cooper, M.D.	$2.25
☐	12737	**THE ALL-IN-ONE CARBOHYDRATE GRAM COUNTER,** Jean Carper	$1.95
☐	12415	**WHICH VITAMINS DO YOU NEED?** Martin Ebon	$2.25
☐	12107	**WHOLE EARTH COOKBOOK,** Cadwallader and Ohr	$1.95
☐	10865	**FASTING AS A WAY OF LIFE,** Allan Cott, M.D.	$1.75
☐	12718	**THE ALL-IN-ONE CALORIE COUNTER,** Jean Carper	$1.95
☐	11402	**THE FAMILY GUIDE TO BETTER FOOD AND BETTER HEALTH,** Ron Deutsch	$2.25
☐	12023	**PSYCHODIETETICS,** Cheraskin, et al.	$2.25

Buy them at your local bookstores or use this handy coupon for ordering:

DO IT!
ALL BY YOURSELF!

☐ 12419	THE BANTAM BOOK OF CORRECT LETTER WRITING	$2.25
☐ 12368	AMY VANDERBILT'S EVERYDAY ETIQUETTE	$2.50
☐ 12258	SOULE'S DICTIONARY OF ENGLISH SYNONYMS	$1.95
☐ 12181	BETTER HOMES AND GARDENS HANDYMAN BOOK	$2.25
☐ 12183	THE ART OF MIXING DRINKS	$1.95
☐ 10507	THE 1977/78 CB GUIDE	$1.50
☐ 12327	THE MOTHER EARTH NEWS HANDBOOK OF HOMEMADE POWER	$2.50
☐ 2903	PROPAGATING HOUSE PLANTS	$1.95
☐ 10932	HOW TO BUY STOCKS 6th rev. ed.	$1.95
☐ 11757	THE HOME COMPUTER HANDBOOK	$2.95

Buy them at your local bookstore or use this handy coupon for ordering:

Bantam Book Catalog

Here's your up-to-the-minute listing of over 1,400 titles by your favorite authors.

This illustrated, large format catalog gives a description of each title. For your convenience, it is divided into categories in fiction and non-fiction—gothics, science fiction, westerns, mysteries, cookbooks, mysticism and occult, biographies, history, family living, health, psychology, art.

So don't delay—take advantage of this special opportunity to increase your reading pleasure.

Just send us your name and address and 50¢ (to help defray postage and handling costs).